Family Time with GOD

Bible Story Activities for Every Day

Compiled and edited by Peg Augustine

 Abingdon Press

FAMILY TIME WITH GOD
Bible Story Activities for Every Day

Copyright © 2001 by Abingdon Press

All rights reserved.
No part of this work may be reproduced or transmitted in any form or by any means, electronic or mechanical, including photocopying and recording, or by an information storage or retrieval system, except as may be expressly permitted by the 1976 Copyright Act or in writing from the publisher. Requests for permission should be addressed to
Abingdon Press, 201 Eighth Avenue South, P. O. Box 801, Nashville, TN 37202

ISBN 0-687-04823-0

Scripture quotations are from the New Revised Standard Version of the Bible, copyright © 1989 by the Division of Christian Education of the National Council of the Churches of Christ in the United States of America. Used by permission.

Stories are adapted from NEW INVITATION: ONE ROOM SUNDAY SCHOOL, REPRODUCIBLE ACTIVITIES. © 1994, 1995, 1996, 1997 Cokesbury. Used by permission.

The recipe for Manna found on page 47 is from **Flood Punch, Bowl Bread, and Group Soup,**
© 2001 by Lisa Flynn and Barbara Younger and published by Abingdon Press. Used by permission

05 06 07 08 09 10 — 10 9 8 7 6 5 4 3 2

PRINTED IN THE UNITED STATES OF AMERICA

Contents

Introduction

There is no greater joy for families than learning about God's Word together. Making the Bible come alive for children and helping them see the connection between well-loved Bible characters and themselves and their family is a great experience. *Family Time With God* will help you create within your family a time, a place, and a way of sharing your own faith journey with your children. Here you will find a year's worth of stories and an activity for every day. Talk points give you a way to hone in on the important biblical truth and its meaning for modern life.

Before each week, read the story and the related activities. It may be that you will not have time for every activity or that your family may want to spend more than one evening on a certain activity. That's just fine. The book gives you a chance to tailor the experience to fit your family. You might want to read through the activities as a family and decide together which activities you will do.

Some days you will need simple supplies or ingredients to make a food item. Some days the book may invite you to take a walk or a drive. All of the activities are suggested to help families grow closer together and help family members learn to apply the experiences and lessons of Bible characters to their own lives. You may want to read the weeks in the order they are written or pick and chose depending on the season of the year or even what is happening in your family at a given time. If you do use the stories in the order in which they are written, the progression helps children see that the promises made in the Old Testament come to pass in the birth, life, and resurrection of Jesus Christ in the New Testament.

In the Beginning

Scripture:
Genesis 1:1-10, 14-19
Psalm 8:1

Talk Point:
God created the heavens and the earth—everything in all creation. We praise God for creation and enjoy the wonder of the universe.

In the beginning,
Before there was anything else,
There was darkness,
And there was God.

Then God created light.
God saw that it was good.
Now there was darkness, called Night,
And there was light, called Day,
And there was God.

And God created two great lights:
The sun to rule the day,
And the moon to rule the night.
God saw that it was good.
Now there was Night, and there was Day.
Now there were sun and moon and stars,
And there was God.

God saw that there was water everywhere,
Rolling, cold, deep, dark water.
So God created the sky to separate the waters:
The deep blue sky, the bright orange sky, the sky that turns
   yellow and purple and pink.
God saw that it was good.
Now there was Night, and there was Day.
Now there were sun and moon and stars.
Now there was sky,
And there was God.

But the world was not finished yet.
God caused dry land to appear out of the water:
Great high mountains, hot dry deserts,
Rolling hills and wide prairies, seashores with sandy beaches,
And fertile soil for growing plants.
God saw that it was good.
Now there was Night, and there was Day.
Now there were sun and moon and stars.
Now there was sky.
Now there were seas and earth,
And there was God.

Day 1 Read the story together. Invite your children to say "And there was God," with you at the appropriate time. Encourage everyone to draw a picture of his or her favorite part of creation. Cover the pictures with wax paper or clear self-adhesive paper and use them as placemats for the next few weeks.

Day 2 Sit outside on the ground. Close your eyes. Listen and smell for a minute or two. Then talk about what you heard, smelled, and felt. Talk about the wonder of God's creation even beyond what you can see.

Day 3 Go to the library together to find a book about stars. After dark lie on a blanket outside with your feet toward the north. Find constellations in the nighttime sky.

Day 4 Let your family enjoy a moonlight walk. Talk about how God's world looks by moonlight. Notice the sky, the clouds, and the moon. What strange shapes do you see? Listen. Do you hear any animals, water, or the wind? How is nighttime different from daytime?

Day 5 Remind your family that God created the earth. Give thanks together. If you live near mountains, thank God for the mountains. If you live near a beach, thank God for the ocean. If you live in a desert, thank God for the sun and the sand. Wherever you live, thank God together for the sun, the moon, and the stars.

Day 6 As a family write a prayer of thanksgiving for God's world. Be sure each person has an opportunity to add a line about his or her favorite part of the natural world.

Day 7 Make sunshine biscuits or cookies. Shape refrigerator biscuits or cookie dough into the shapes of the sun, moon, and stars. For sunshine biscuits melt cheese on top of the biscuits just before they are done. For sunshine cookies decorate with yellow frosting.

Plants

Scripture:
Genesis 1:11-13

Talk Point:
God made plants grow to meet the needs of people and animals. We thank God for the many ways plants make our lives better.

"Then God said, 'Let the earth put forth vegetation: plants yielding seed, and fruit trees of every kind on earth that bear fruit with the seed in it.' And it was so," said the storyteller.

Josh loved to hear the stories. But plants? What difference does it make that God created plants? *What good are all these plants for, anyway?* he thought.

"We use the plants that God created every day," he heard the storyteller continue. "When we ate our meal tonight, we ate plants—lettuce, cucumbers, beans, and wheat bread. The fig cakes made with honey are my favorite. Later tonight I plan to have a snack of pistachio nuts."

Yes, thought Josh, *that was a good meal. I guess I never thought about foods being plants.*

The storyteller continued, "And look at this tunic I'm wearing. This cloth was woven after the flax leaves were dried and then spun to make thread."

I have clothes made from flax, thought Josh. *Is that a plant?*

"Just last week," the storyteller said, "Rachel was sick. But she's better now. The barley porridge was just what she needed!"

I had a mixture of palm leaves once for a stomachache, Josh remembered. *Maybe plants really are important.*

Josh began listening now. He wanted to know more about the plants God created for people to use. The storyteller told about so many plants that Josh began to lose count, but he remembered about using reeds to measure distance and to make baskets. He remembered trees where birds build nests, and branches that are used to make shelters, and lilies and crocuses that make the fields so beautiful.

Well, thought Josh, *plants are important!*

When the storyteller was finished, Josh left the campfire remembering the storyteller's words: "The earth brought forth vegetation: plants yielding seed of every kind, and trees of every kind bearing fruit with the seed in it. And God saw that it was good."

"I'm going to eat a plant now," said Josh. "In fact, I may eat several. I want almonds and grapes and maybe even some cantaloupe!"

Day 1 As you plant some bulbs outside (or in a pot, if it is winter), talk about God's plan for the world. Encourage family members to talk about their favorite plants. If you are planting the bulbs inside in winter, discuss what you will do with the pots when they flower.

Day 2 Make a snack that uses only plants—celery, carrots, raisins, nuts, dried fruits, banana chips, and so forth. Talk about the plants God created and the many ways we use them.

Day 3 Look for seeds at home. How many can you find in your refrigerator or in your cabinets?

Day 4 Plant a sweet potato and watch it grow. Stick toothpicks around the edge and suspend the potato over a jar of water so that the bottom of the sweet potato touches the water. As the water evaporates, add more water. As you and your child watch the sweet potato vine grow, talk about how God creates plants from seeds, bulbs, or tubers.

Day 5 Let your child adopt a tree (or a bush or other plant). Work together to learn as much as possible about the tree. What kind is it? Does it like lots of sun or not? How deep do its roots go? Is it healthy? Do insects or birds live in the tree? How does the tree sound when the wind blows? Does the tree have blooms? Do they smell good?

Day 6 Make a cactus garden. Sprinkle small rocks in the bottom of a shallow bowl. Fill the bowl with sand. Plant two or three cactus plants. Sprinkle the garden with water and keep it on a windowsill. Talk about the variety of plants God has created.

Day 7 Try a water experiment: Cut a warm, boiled potato in half. Put each half in the bottom of a quart jar. Add clean water to one jar. Cover about half of the potato. Label the jar "Clean Water." Cover half of the potato in the second jar with water in which you have washed your dirty hands. Label the jar "Dirty Water." Cover the jars and place them in a warm dark place.

Check the jars after a few days to see what has happened. Think about it: What happens to plants and animals when the water in our lakes and streams becomes polluted? Decide to do what you can to keep the water clean.

Living Creatures!

Talk Point:
God created different kinds of animals—all living creatures. We praise God for creation as we enjoy and care for animals.

God looked around at all that had been created. There was day and night. There was sky and sea. There was earth. The sky filled with clouds. The sea rolled and crashed against the land. The earth was covered with many growing plants. And God said, "This is good. But it is not finished yet. I must have living creatures."

"Let the waters be filled with living creatures," God said. And fish appeared—big fish, little fish, short and fat fish, long and skinny fish, bluefish, red fish, yellow fish, striped fish, speckled fish, prickly fish, and slimy fish. And God said, "This is good, but it is not finished yet."

God said, "Let the earth be filled with living creatures." And it was so. There were big birds, little birds, short and fat birds, tall and thin birds, birds with short legs, birds with long legs, birds with almost no legs at al. There were birds that could fly very high and even birds that could not fly at all. There were birds that walked, birds that ran, and birds that swam. There were red birds, blue birds, yellow birds, and birds with many colors. And God said, "This is good. But it is not finished yet."

"I want many kinds of animals," God said. And it was so. There were big animals, little animals, short and fat animals, and tall and thin animals. There were animals with four legs, animals with six legs, animals with eight legs, animals with no legs, and animals that had so many legs it was impossible to count them all. There were animals with fur, animals with shells, animals with scales, and animals no one would want to touch to find out what they were made of. There were animals that walked, animals that ran, animals that flew, animals that crawled, animals that slithered, and animals that hardly moved at all. And God said, "This is good. That's enough for now."

And God said to the fish, to the birds, and to the animals, "Go make more of your own kind. Fill the earth!" And it was so.

Day 1 Take a walk in your neighborhood, in a park, or in a camping area. Count the many kinds of plants and animals you see. Can you name each one?

Day 2 Go to a pet store. Admire the birds, the fish, the ferrets, the mice, and the other animals you see there. Thank God for animals of all kinds. Perhaps you could take a bag of cat or dog food to an animal shelter.

Day 3 Feed the birds in your yard. String popped corn, cranberries, raisins, cheese, and dried fruit on a thread and hang it from a tree limb.

Day 4 Visit an aquarium. Talk about all the different kinds of fish God made. If this is not practical, find books in the library about fish, or look up a particular kind of fish on the Internet. (Your older children might be interested in looking up whales and sharks and seeing what the differences are in these two ocean dwelling creatures.)

Day 5 Keep a journal of the animals you see near your home during the week. Encourage your children to draw pictures of the animals. Go to the library or use the Internet to find about more about the animals in your area. If your ancestors came from another country, find out about the animals that live there. Talk about how animals adapt to the conditions of the places they live. Find books or an Internet source about animals in Australia.

Day 6 Watch a bed of ants. Give the ants crumbs of bread and watch what happens. Be careful, though. Do not leave your child alone with the ants. Remind your family that God planned for ants to live together in colonies, helping one another. How does your own family help one another? Thank God for families.

Day 7 If there is a petting zoo nearby, take your child to visit. Help your child develop an appreciation for all of God's animals. If this is not practical, let everyone bring his or her favorite stuffed animal to a meal and tell as much as he or she knows about the animal it represents. Thank God for animals and for the pleasure they give us.

It All Works Together!

Talk Point:
God created an orderly and dependable world. Children can learn to trust God as they see God's plan in the succession of day and night and in the cycle of the seasons.

God looked at the plants and the animals that had been created and said, 'It is good!'"

It's about time! thought Joel. *Nothing has gone right all day. I want to get this over with and go home. I hope the storyteller doesn't have a long story tonight.*

"But God knew that if the world would always be good, there must be some order," continued the storyteller. "There must be things that people could depend on day after day and season after season. So God gave order to the seasons, to the ways plants grow, and to the weather. And God saw that the order was good.

"We can depend on God," the storyteller said. "God created an orderly world. Even when things seem to go wrong, we can depend on God.

"Did you ever know a time when day did not come after night? Was there ever a time when fall came after winter and there was no spring or summer? Was there ever a time when no food grew anywhere on the earth? Was there ever a spring when the flowers did not bloom or the birds did not sing?

"Oh, yes," said the storyteller. "There are days when everything seems to go wrong. Our lives are filled with challenges. But we can depend on God's world to provide the things we need. There will always be plants for food and plants for building our homes. Animals will always be here to provide food and clothing and to help us with our work. We can depend on God's world. Even though some days might not be exactly the way we want them to be, we do know that we can depend of God's world. We know that:

> As long as the earth endures,
>   seedtime and harvest, cold and heat,
> summer and winter, day and night,
>   shall not cease." (Genesis 8:22)

The storyteller's story was short tonight. But Joel didn't mind staying at the campfire a little longer. It had been a bad day. But things didn't seem so bad anymore as Joel listened to the sounds of God's world. He knew he would hear the wind blowing in the trees. He knew he would hear insects singing. He knew it was a lizard he heard running through the fallen leaves. It was night, and Joel knew that tomorrow would come, and God's world would be filled with life for another day.

Day 1 Help your child collect items to contribute to an organization that provides help for victims of natural disasters. Talk about being prepared to help others.

Day 2 Look at the foods in your pantry. Can you name where each kind of food is grown? Perhaps the label will tell you. At mealtime, give thanks for the people who helped to grow your food.

Day 3 Find a stream of water. Hike upstream to find the source. Talk about how all parts of God's world are linked and orderly. If this is not possible, check out a book about a river and learn about its source and about the places it flows through. Or look up a particular river on the Internet. What happens when the river overflows its banks? Reassure your child that even when bad things happen, we can depend of God and on God's world.

Day 4 Take a hike together. How many kinds of life can you see? Are there young trees growing near old trees? Are there bird nests with eggs? Are there grown birds? What other kinds of plants and animals do you see? How do they depend on one another? If a hike isn't possible, watch a nature show together on television. See how many ways you can name that plants and animals depend on each other.

Day 5 Talk about ways the members of your family depend on one another. How do parents help children? How do children help parents? What things do parents and children do together? Thank God for your family.

Day 6 Play "What would happen if . . ." Discuss the benefits and problems if: water flowed uphill instead of downhill; we got younger each year instead of older; rain came up from the ground; the sun shone for one hour at a time and then it was dark for a week; we ate dessert before eating the rest of the meal.

Day 7 Read Ecclesiastes 3:14 together. Thank God that the world God created has endured and will continue to endure.

Caretakers

In the beginning, before there was anything else, there was God.

Then God began to create. God created day and night. God created sky, sea, and earth. God created the sun, the moon, and the stars. God created plants. God created fish and birds and animals of every sort.

When God looked at all that had been created, God said, "It is good. But it is not finished yet."

Once again God created. This time God created human beings—male and female. And God blessed them, because they were special.

God said to the human beings, "I have a job for you. Look around. Everything you see belongs to me, but I am giving it to you. You will take care of it for me. Have many children. Live in every place that can be lived in. I am putting you in charge. You are in charge of the sky, the sea, and the earth. You are in charge of the fish, the birds, and all the world animals. You will take care of everything I have created."

The humans were nervous. "How can we be in charge? There is so much to take care of. How will we know what to do?"

"We will work together," God promised. "I will always be there with you. All you have to do is ask. There is nothing we cannot do if we work together."

And so human beings took charge of God's wonderful world. Most of the time human beings are mindful of their job. They take good care of God's creation, and everything goes smoothly.

But sometimes human beings get so busy doing other things that they forget the job that God has given them. They make mistakes. They do not take good care of God's creation. Then it is time for human beings to remember what God has said: "There is nothing we cannot do when we work together. I will always be there with you."

And so human beings, with God's help, keep on learning how to be caretakers of God's creation.

Day 1
Clean out a closet or a room together. Put things that do not go back on the shelves or in the closet in boxes labeled "Give Away," "Throw Away," and "fix." Be sure to take care of the things in the boxes.

Day 2
Give your child responsibility for watering plants, feeding pets, or taking out the trash. Remind your child that these jobs are part of taking care of God's world! Perhaps you can work together, talking about the wonder of creation and the wonder of God as you work. Design a special checklist with the jobs listed to keep on the door or another place. Encourage your child to put Psalm 8:6a somewhere on the checklist and to be creative as he or she designs the list.

Day 3
Does your family recycle? If not, find out where recycling is available in your community. Talk with your family about recycling as one way to care for God's world. Set aside an area for storing recyclables. If you have to take items to a central dropoff point, do it once a month or so as a family. Make it a special day.

Day 4
If your family enjoyed feeding the birds a few weeks ago, add a permanent bird feeder to your yard. You may want to buy a bird feeder to fill with seed, or you can make a feeder of your own. It may simply be a tin plate filled with bird seed and set on a fence post where birds can find it. Start keeping a journal of the different birds your family sees there at different times of the day. Perhaps you would like to buy a book of birds in your area so that you can identify them. Encourage your children to draw pictures of the birds. Use their artwork to send notes to grandparents and other family members.

Day 5
As a family write a letter to a representative or a senator in your state. Tell about your interest in taking care of the earth. Encourage your elected official to vote in favor of laws that will protect the earth.

Day 6
If your family has a garden, begin a compost pile. If you already have a compost pile, find ways to let your child help. If you do not have a garden, begin growing some small pots of herbs in your kitchen window. Use the herbs in cooking. You might also dry some of them to make potpourri.

Day 7
Read Psalm 104:1-31a, a psalm of praise to the Creator, together. Have a strong reader read each verse or sentence. Ask the other family members to say verse 31a, "May the glory of the Lord endure forever," at the end of each verse or sentence.

Free to Choose

Scripture:
Genesis 2:8-9, 15-17;
3:1-13, 22-23
Psalm 100:3

Talk Point:
God has given human beings the freedom of choose between good and evil. Christians try to choose what is good. When we do make wrong choices, God will forgive us.

When God created the first people, Adam and Eve, God placed them in a beautiful garden. God said, "Take care of my garden. Eat from any of the trees except the tree of the knowledge of good and evil. If you eat from that tree, you will die."

Adam and Eve quickly agreed. After all, there were so many other things to eat that they could not imagine needing to eat from that tree. So, things went well in the garden—for a while.

Then one day while Eve was walking in the garden, she passed the special tree. The fruit looked sweet and good.

Then Eve heard a voice close to her ear. "Just taste the fruit. It looks awfully good." Eve looked around and saw a serpent.

"It does look good," Eve agreed, "but God told us not to eat from this tree. If we do, we will die."

"Oh, that's silly! God just said that to keep you away from the tree. You will not die. In fact, if you eat this fruit, you will become as wise as God. Don't you want to be as wise as God?" the serpent asked.

Eve thought for a moment. She wanted to do as God said. But she also wanted to be wise. So she picked a fruit from the tree and took a big bite. Later she gave it to Adam, who also ate the fruit.

As soon as they had eaten the fruit, Adam and Eve knew that they had made a bad choice. *What will happen to us?* they wondered.

Their question was soon answered. When they heard God walking in the garden, they hid. But God called out to them. God knew they had disobeyed.

God spoke with sadness, "I have created a special place for you. I have given you everything you could possibly want. And yet you have chosen to do the one thing I told you not to do. Now you can no longer live in the special garden I have created for you. In order to eat, you will have to grown your own food. Life will be hard now. I gave you freedom to choose. You have chosen unwisely. Now you must live with the consequences."

Day 1 Give your children opportunities to make choices. Let them choose the menu for supper one night, which book to read at bedtime, or which game to play. Be sure that any of the choices you provide will be acceptable to the whole family. Or plan a family picnic together. Let each family member be responsible for specific choices. For example: Where will you go? What food will you take? What else will you do together while you are gone? (Too cold for a picnic? Try having one on the floor in the living room.)

Day 2 Let your family list possible choices of TV programs to watch. Talk about what makes a good choice or a bad choice. Talk about choices that parents make for children. Which choices will the children be able to make alone someday?

Day 3 Learn Psalm 100:3 together. Talk about the responsibilities we have because we are God's people.

Day 4 Do an experiment. Fill a bucket with water. Drop in some dirt, twigs, a candy wrapper, a bottle cap, some pebbles, food coloring, and cooking oil. Then try to remove the pollution. Use a spoon, a strainer, or tongs. Can the pollution be completely cleaned up? No, not even with the most modern water-cleaning methods. Talk with your child about why it is important to choose to avoid pollution in the first place.

Day 5 Check the cabinets in your home. What products do you have that can be harmful to the environment? Have your family make a list together of new choices of products to use.

Day 6 Tell your child about a time you had an important choice to make. If you made a good choice, tell what happened. If you made a bad choice, explain what you learned.

Day 7 Write a family prayer. Thank God for giving people freedom to make choices, for being with us when we have choices to make, and for loving us no matter what choices we make. Share your prayer with another family.

It's Going to Rain!

When God created the world, everything was good. But after a while the people forgot about God. They forgot who had created them and the world around them. All the people forgot about God—all except Noah and Noah's family.

"Noah," said God, "I am not happy with the way things are on the earth. The people mistreat one another—all of them except you and your family. Noah, I want to start all over again. I want you to build a boat. A big boat. I will send a flood to destroy the earth. But you and your family will be safe."

So Noah and his family began to build a big boat. When the boat was finished, God said, "Noah, fill the boat with animals. Take two of every kind of animal on earth."

So Noah gathered animals. There were elephants and kangaroo, tigers and chimpanzees, rhinoceros and giraffes, parakeets and camels, fleas and butterflies, snails and rabbits, turtles and alligators.

When everyone and everything was safe inside the boat, rain began to fall. It rained for forty days. The boat began to float. Higher and higher the water came until it covered everything, even the tallest mountain. Winds rocked the boat. But Noah, his family, and all the animals were safe and dry—because Noah was faithful to God.

Then one day the boat stopped rocking. Everything was still. Noah opened a window and sent out a raven. She stretched her wings and took off. But there was no place for her to land. So she came back to the boat. Seven days later Noah opened the window again. This time he sent out a dove, but again the dove came back.

After another seven days Noah sent the dove out a second time. When she returned, she was carrying a fresh olive leaf. Noah knew the water had gone down.

After another week Noah sent the dove out again, and she did not return. Then God spoke to Noah. "Leave the ark," God said. "Take your family and all the animals onto the dry land."

Noah built an altar to praise God for keeping them safe. Then a beautiful sight appeared in the sky. "It is a rainbow," God said. "It is a sign of my promise to you and to all living things. I will never again send a flood to destroy the earth. Remember my promise."

Day 1 Paint pictures with water on a sidewalk or patio outside. Provide a bucket of water and a large paintbrush. Remember together that God created water. Talk about the animals that live in water. Talk about how water is important to your family.

Day 2 Share a snack of animal crackers and cold water. Talk about making choices. Encourage your children to think about what God would want each time there is a decision to be made.

Day 3 Make a wave model together. Fill a quart jar one third full with vegetable oil. Add water to fill the jar almost full. Add blue food coloring. Add a cork if one is available. Close the jar securely. Turn the jar on its side. Move it gently from side to side to see the wave in motion. Think of the cork as Noah's ark floating on the waves.

Day 4 Keep a weather calendar for several weeks. Draw a picture on each day to record the weather that day—a sun, raindrops, clouds, leaves blowing, and so forth. Talk about how the changes in the weather make it possible for the world to change and to grow just as God planned.

Day 5 Make rainbow cookies. Divide sugar cookie dough into four parts. Add food coloring to make each part a different rainbow color. Shape each color into a four-inch wide rectangle that is about one-fourth inch thick. Stack the pieces and press down to make them stick together. Wrap in waxed paper and chill for two hours. Cut into one-fourth-inch thick slices. Shape the slices into rainbow shapes. Bake at 375 degrees on an ungreased baking sheet for seven minutes.

Day 6 Talk about promises you and your child make. Promise to help each other remember that it is important to keep promises. Think of someone who has kept a promise to your family. Make a certificate for that person. Include Genesis 9:13 and a rainbow.

Day 7 Make rainbows and talk about how rainbows remind us that God has promised to take care of the world.

> Blow bubbles to find rainbows.
> Squirt food coloring in rainbow colors into a pan of water. Add a drop of liquid detergent.
> Stand with your back to the sun. Make a fine spray with a water hose. Look at a forty-five degree angle to see a rainbow. (Hint: Try early morning or late afternoon.)
> Put a full glass of water where the sun can shine directly on the clear glass. Lay a sheet of paper on the floor. Look for the rainbow in the paper.

Lisa's Move

Talk Point:
God called Abraham and his family to go to a new country and to be God's people. Abraham obeyed, and God was with him. God will always be with us.

It's just not fair," said Lisa. "I don't want to move. I don't want to leave our church. I don't want to go to another school."

"I know," said her dad. "Sometimes I feel that way too. But when a pastor moves to a new church, it is for a good reason. We love our church here, but now we must move on. It is part of our covenant."

Lisa stamped her foot. "I don't like your old covenant." Dad lifted Lisa to his knee and reached for his Bible.

"Listen to a story about a family who moved a long way," he said.

"Abraham was born in the city of Ur, a busy place near two rivers. People from all over the known world came to Ur to buy and to sell. One day Abraham's father said, 'We must move to Haran.' So the whole family moved.

"They walked, taking their possessions with them. At Haran they found another busy city, this time a caravan center. There Terah, Abraham's father, died. Abraham became the head of the family.

"One day God spoke to Abraham. It is here in the Bible: 'Now the LORD said to Abram, "Go from your country and your kindred and your father's house to the land that I will show you. I will make of you a great nation, and I will bless you, and make your name great, so that you will be a blessing. . . ." So Abram went as the LORD had told him; and Lot went with him. Abram was seventy-five years old when he departed from Haran. Abram took his wife Sarai and his brother's son Lot, and all the possessions that they had gathered . . . and they set forth to go to the land of Canaan' (Genesis 12:1-2, 4-5).

"God and Abraham had a covenant, a solemn agreement," Lisa's dad continued. "Abraham obeyed God, moving to a far country. God promised to be with Abraham forever and to bless his family."

"Did you make a covenant with God?" asked Lisa.

"Oh, yes," answered her dad. "I promised God to serve in our church wherever God called me. God promised to be present with me and to help me."

Then I guess we'll have to move," said Lisa thoughtfully. "At least we won't have to walk!"

Day 1

Find Iraq, Turkey, Palestine, and Israel on a present-day map. Compare this to the area known as Mesopotamia and Canaan in Abraham's time. If these countries are mentioned in the news, talk to your family about what is happening there.

Day 2

Talk about the differences between now and when Grandma was young. Remind your family that through all these times, people have known that God is with them, and God's people have sought to be obedient to God.

Day 3

Read Genesis 12:2. List how each member of the family may be a blessing this week.

Day 4

Talk about the ways families and friends cared for one another in Bible times. Check out a book from the public library or your church library that will help children see how life was lived when Abraham took his long journey.

Day 5

There were many important covenants made in Bible times. Look up these Bible references to see who made the covenants: Exodus 19:5-6; Genesis 9:11; Genesis 12:1-2; Psalm 132:12.

Day 6

Look at pictures in your family album. Talk about how each person has grown and changed over the years. Say a prayer of thanks for God's wonderful plan. If you have moved over the years, remember good times from earlier days. Write a note to old friends. Remind your family that God has promised to always be with us, no matter where we live.

Day 7

Talk more about how life is different today than it was in Bible times. Ask each family member to decide what he or she would miss most if he or she had to live as people did then. Recall earlier devotions and stories that told of how we are to care for the earth. Plan a family "hunger meal." Either skip a meal (not a good idea with very young children), or prepares something simple and inexpensive. Donate the money you save to a hunger project.

Sarah's Wondrous Thing

Scripture:
Genesis 18:1-14;
21:1-7
Psalm 72:18

Talk Point:
God kept the promise to make Abraham and Sarah's family a great nation. God always keeps promises—even promises that seem impossible to us.

My name is Sarah. My husband is Abraham. One day God called Abraham to move to a far country. God promised Abraham land and many descendants. God said that Abraham would be a blessing to all the people of the world.

Naturally we expected a baby to be born soon. How else would Abraham have many descendants? But the years passed. In a time of famine we went to Egypt. When we returned, we had more sheep and goats and camels and tents than ever. But we still did not have any land, and we had no baby! I was ready to believe that God did not mean those promises at all. One day when I was very old and discouraged, a strange thing happened. I was in the tent directing the servants in all the household chores. Abraham was sleeping by the door of the tent when he noticed we had company. How puzzled he was! He had not seen a caravan arrive; the servants had not come to warn him that travelers were approaching. Nevertheless, Abraham jumped up and ran to the visitors. He greeted them kindly and called to the servants to bring water for their feet. He told me to make bread. Then Abraham ran to the herd to choose a calf to prepare a feast for the visitors. Travelers in the desert are always helped and treated with great courtesy.

I listened to everything from inside the tent. When I heard one of the visitors say, "Your wife, Sarah, shall have a son," I began to laugh. Me! I was eighty-nine years old!

The visitor said, "Is anything too wonderful for the Lord?" Then Abraham and I realized that what our visitors said was true. I began to look forward to having a wondrous baby, even though I was old.

Sure enough, a year later God gave us the promised baby boy. We named him Isaac, which means "laughter." My heart was warm and happy. I was now ninety years old. Abraham was one hundred years old! It was a miracle. Now I know that I should have trusted God's promise from the very beginning. God can do wondrous things.

Day 1 Talk about the story. Sarah was ninety years old when Isaac was born. That may not seem like a miracle to the very youngest children, but older ones will find it awesome. God was bringing about the founding of a new people, God's chosen people, through whom God intended to bless the whole world. Remind your family that we are God's heirs to that blessing in the person of Jesus Christ. Children love to hear about their own births. Talk about how eagerly you waited for each birth. If you have some of their baby clothes, show them.

Day 2 Draw squares on a large sheet of paper to represent a couple of weeks or a month. Wrapping paper or butcher paper from the store will work fine. Encourage your family to draw pictures each day that represent promises of God. Or cut pictures from magazines and paste them in the squares. Try to do one each day. This will encourage an attitude of awareness and gratitude for God's promises.

Day 3 A family tree was very important to Abraham and Sarah. Family records were essential to Bible characters. Families were valued and cherished. Think about your own family and begin to make a family tree that shows your children's parents, grandparents, and great-grandparents. Point out that Sarah had her baby when she was older than most great-grandparents, and when Abraham was one hundred years old.

Day 4 What hopes and promises has your family experienced through the generations? How has God blessed your family? Do you know the country where your ancestors came from? Find the country on a map and use an encyclopedia or the Internet to find out more about the country.

Day 5 Encourage each family member to draw two pictures—one of a promise God made to the individual and one that the individual has made to God. If your children have grandparents or other older relatives, send the pictures to them with an explanation.

Day 6 Start a scrapbook called "A Book of Wondrous Things." Try to add to it at least once a month. Let everyone have a hand in designing the cover. Encourage your children to draw pictures of how God has blessed your family.

Day 7 Go to the library and check out books about the country of your ancestors. Is your country mentioned in the Bible? Use an almanac or the internet to find out how to get tourist information about the country. Write for information and plan a pretend visit. Make up passports for each family member. Let family members choose places they would like to visit. Set an itinerary. Thank God for the care God gives the earth and for putting us in families.

A Growing Family

Scripture:
Genesis 24:1-67;
25:19-28

Talk Point:
Through Isaac, Jacob, and Esau God continued to keep the promise to bless Abraham's family. As our family changes, God is with us, still loving us.

Isaac was forty years old. His mother, Sarah, had died a few years ago. It was customary at that time for parents to choose marriage partners for their sons and daughters. Abraham needed to find a wife for Isaac.

Abraham always remembered the covenant. He wanted to be sure that Isaac's wife would honor and follow God. He wanted a wife for Isaac from his own land and his own people.

Abraham sent a loyal servant to find a wife for Isaac. When the servant arrived outside the city of Nahor, where some of Abraham's kindred lived, it was time for the women to draw water from the well. The servant prayed that God would make his search successful. "Let the girl to whom I say, 'Please offer your jar that I may drink,' and who shall say, 'Drink, and I will water your camels'—let her be the one whom you have appointed for your servant Isaac."

Before he had finished his prayer, a lovely woman named Rebekah approached. Everything happened just as the servant had prayed! Then the servant gave Rebekah a gold ring and some bracelets. He returned with her to her father and brother, who agreed that Rebekah was certainly God's choice as a wife for Isaac. The servant praised God.

The servant did not wish to delay the journey back to Abraham and Isaac. Rebekah was willing to start immediately for her new home. Several servants were allowed to go with her. The whole caravan started back to Canaan.

By this time Isaac was settled in the Negeb. One evening he was out walking in his fields when the caravan approached. Isaac knew that this was the woman God had led Abraham and the servant to choose for his wife. He took Rebekah to his mother's tent, the very one where Sarah had laughed when the angel said she would have a son. There Isaac and Rebekah made their home.

Even when Isaac and Rebekah did not have children for many years, Isaac did not doubt the covenant or the faithfulness of God. He prayed for children. Finally twins were born to Rebekah and Isaac. Their names were Esau, the firstborn, and Jacob, the younger.

Day 1

Discuss the story. It covers many changes in the life of Abraham and his family. Even good changes can bring stress into a family's life. Talk about changes that have happened in your family. How did Mom and Dad meet? How long was it before children joined the family? Remind your family that God is present in the midst of change and that God works through the ordinary experiences and growth of a family. Encourage family members to draw a picture or to write about some family change. Add those things to your scrapbook.

Day 2

Cut many letters of the alphabet from newspapers or magazines. Place them in a paper sack. Let each person draw a letter. Use the letters to remind you of the names of Abraham's family, your family, books of the Bible, or a familiar Bible verse.

Day 3

Sarah named her baby Isaac because the name means "laughter." Talk about how names were chosen for your family members. If someone was named for an older relative who is still living, take a picture and send it to that relative. Go to the mailbox as a family to post the letter. Thank God for families, near and far.

Day 4

Write a *cinquain*—a poem with five lines—for each person's name. One popular form of cinquains follows this pattern: Line 1 is the title and subject of the poem (one word, the person's name). Line 2 describes the subject (two words). Line 3 has action words about the subject (three words). Line 4 describes a feeling about the subject (four words). Line 5 is another word that renames the subject or title (one word).

Day 5

Consult a Bible-times book about how people traveled in Isaac's day. If you were traveling to live in a new place and you had to go by camel caravan, what things would you need to leave behind? Let each person choose one thing that he or she just couldn't live without. Would it be possible to take it along?

Day 6

Continue to talk about Bible times travel. Let each person make up a sound (camels walking, tents blowing in the breeze, and so forth), and let others guess what the sound is. Thank God for sounds and for the gift of hearing.

Day 7

Has your family seen people who do not have homes? Does your church provide any support programs for people who do not have homes? Plan a way for your family to help.

Jacob, the Trickster

Scripture:
Genesis 25:29-34;
27:1-45

Talk Point:
God did not save Jacob from the consequences of cheating Esau, but God helped Jacob in his trouble. When we do wrong, God still loves us and will be with us.

Jacob and Esau were different. Esau was a rugged, hairy man who loved to hunt. Jacob was a quiet man who preferred tending the flocks. As the oldest son Esau was entitled to many of his father's possessions once Isaac died. This was called a birthright.

One day Esau came home from hunting and asked Jacob to share the soup he was making.

"I'll give you some soup," Jacob said, "if you will give me your birthright."

"My birthright!" Esau exclaimed.

"Sure," said Jacob, "I would like to have the honors of the firstborn. What about it?"

Esau shrugged, "Oh, all right. What is a birthright if I starve to death?"

Even though Esau had sold his birthright he was still entitled to a special blessing from his father. But Rebekah wanted Jacob to have that as well. She knew that Isaac had sent Esau out to hunt for game to make a savory stew and that once he had eaten, Isaac would give Esau his blessing.

"Jacob," Rebekah said, "I want you to have the blessing, and not your brother. Go quickly to the herd and get me two choice goats. I will prepare food for your father. When you take it to him, he will give you the blessing."

"This will not work!" exclaimed Jacob. "Esau is a hairy man, and I have smooth skin. When my father touches me, he will know the difference and will curse me."

But Rebekah insisted. While Jacob got the goats, she took some of Esau's clothing for Jacob to wear. She prepared savory food and bread. She put the skins of the goats on Jacob's hands and neck so that he would feel like Esau to his father. She sent Jacob to Isaac with the food and bread.

The trick worked, and Isaac blessed Jacob. When Esau found out, he was so angry that Rebekah feared he would kill Jacob. She told Jacob to flee for his life, and he left his home. He never saw his mother again.

Day 1 Make and eat lentil soup. It was probably a soup like this one for which Esau sold his birthright.

Day 2 Talk about how Jacob tricked his brother. Sometimes we like to play practical jokes or April Fools jokes, but anytime a trick or joke hurts another person, it is the wrong thing to do. Encourage family members to act out the story, showing with their faces how Jacob and Esau must have felt at each stage of the story.

Lentil Soup

2 cups dried lentils
8 cups water
1/2 cup each of chopped onion, celery, carrots, and tomatoes
1 cup chopped pre-cooked meat
salt and pepper to taste

Wash and sort the lentils. Put them in a large pot with water, celery, onion, and carrots. Cook until the lentils are tender.
Add tomatoes, meat, and seasonings. Simmer ten minutes.
Serve steaming hot with chunks of bread.

Day 3 Take a trip to the mall and be people watchers. Notice how many races or cultures you see. What are the ages of the people you see? How is each person unique? What image of God do you see in each person?

Day 4 Continue to talk about families in Bible times and today. Ask each family member to place his or her hand and arm on a large piece of brown paper (a grocery bag works well), fingers spread. Let a partner draw around the hand and arm. This forms a tree with a trunk and branches. Cut out leaves from various colors of paper to make leaves for the tree. On each leaf let family members write the name of someone or something to include in their prayers.

Day 5 Talk about the feelings of the people in this week's story. Choose some shaving creams/gels that come in different colors. Squirt a bit of shaving cream on the table in front of each person. Ask each person to think of what it is like to be hurt by another person. Let them fingerpaint the feeling in the shaving cream. Talk about each picture. Then, using wet paper towels, clean up the shaving cream, talking about how God forgives us when we have made wrong choices and how we should ask forgiveness from anyone we have hurt.

Day 6 Make simple cards to exchange with family members. Print "You are a blessing to me" on each card and let each person decorate one to give to another person. Parents may want to give a card to each child and add the reasons why each child is a special blessing.

Day 7 If your family likes to sing, choose a praise song for your family song. Otherwise, work together to write a family cheer.

Esau Forgives Jacob

Scripture:
Genesis 29:1, 13-30;
31:3-7, 17-18;
32:3-21; 33:1-11, 16-20
Psalm 32:1

Talk Point:

When Jacob returned home, he asked God to protect him and his family from Esau's anger. But Esau welcomed Jacob as a brother. With God's help, we can forgive those who have been mean or hurtful, especially when they are sorry.

Jacob's uncle, Laban, greeted him warmly when he arrived in Haran. After a month Laban suggested that Jacob work with Laban's herds for wages. But Jacob had another idea! Jacob had fallen in love with Laban's younger daughter, Rachel. He offered to work for seven years for Laban in return for the privilege of marrying Rachel.

Seven years later Laban gave a great feast to celebrate the marriage. But the bride wore a veil over her face. Jacob did not know until it was too late that Laban had tricked him. The bride was Leah, Rachel's older sister! Now Jacob had to work seven more years to have Rachel as his wife.

Laban's herds grew because Jacob was such a good shepherd, but Jacob was not happy. Laban did not pay him fair wages. Laban's sons were jealous of Jacob, and Jacob's wives and sons were jealous of one another. Jacob was glad when God told him to return with his family to Canaan. But he was worried too. What would Esau do? Did Esau still want to kill him?

As Jacob drew near to Canaan, he sent a messenger to Esau. The messenger returned and told Jacob that Esau was coming to meet him with four hundred men. Jacob was distressed. Would his brother Esau try to kill him and his family?

Jacob prayed. He confessed that he was afraid of Esau. But Jacob remembered the covenant and thanked God for his family and flocks. Then he sent a great number of goats, sheep, camels, cows, and donkeys as gifts to Esau.

Jacob went before his family to meet Esau. When he saw Esau coming, Jacob bowed seven times to show his respect. But Esau ran joyfully to meet his brother! He embraced Jacob and kissed him and wept. He was happy that his brother had returned.

Jacob and Esau parted and settled peacefully in different parts of the land. Jacob pitched his tent in Shechem. There he erected an altar to God in thankfulness for his safe return to his homeland.

Day 1 Learn Psalm 32:1 together. Say it at each mealtime this week.

Day 2 Make friendship bracelets. You will need three different colors of yarn, scissors, rubber bands or string, and masking tape. Cut the yarn into two-feet lengths. Give each person a length of each color yarn. Align the yarn at one end and tie the ends together. Secure the tied end to the table top with a piece of masking tape. Leave about two inches of yarn and tie another knot. Then braid the yarn to create a bracelet. An adult or older child will have to help younger children. When the braid is long enough to go around the wrist comfortably, tie another knot. Cut the yarn about two inches below the knot. Remove the tape from the other end. Cut the initial knot from that end. Use the loose ends to tie the bracelet onto the wrist. You may want to exchange bracelets with other family members.

Day 3 Look in magazines for pictures that show peace or generosity. Cut them out and let each family member add to a small collage to put in your "Wondrous Things" scrapbook. It is a wondrous thing when we can live together in peace.

Day 4 Read some proverbs from the Bible. Many of them deal with living together in harmony. Here are a number that tell how we should act as friends: Proverbs 17:17; Proverbs 12:26; Proverbs 18:24; Proverbs 27:5-6; Proverbs 13:20. Encourage family members to write a proverb of their own.

Day 5 Work together to make a peacemaker acrostic using your family name (if family members have more than one family name, use all the names). Draw enough small boxes vertically on a page to equal the letters in your name. Print each letter of your name in a box. Think of ways your family can be peacemakers that includes one of the letters. Write your ideas on the appropriate lines. Add these pages to your scrapbook or send to a grandparent or other relative.

Day 6 Ask: "How can we use this story in our family life?" The Bible comes alive when children realize that their problems are just like the ones so long ago. God is just as faithful now in giving us help and care as God was for Abraham and his descendants.

Day 7 Say a forgiveness prayer. Someone can read each line, and the rest will respond with "God, forgive."

God, Forgive

Dear God, we do not always do what is right.
Sometimes we say things that aren't nice.
Sometimes we do not share.
Sometimes we disobey our parents.
Sometimes we don't keep our promises.
Sometimes we don't do our very best.
Amen.

Joseph and His Brothers

Scripture:
Genesis 37:1-36; 39:1-3

Talk Point:
God will be with us in the pain and trouble that comes when we or when others have been cruel like Joseph's brothers or thoughtless like Joseph.

Dan: My name is Dan. I am one of Jacob's sons. But not his favorite son—that's Joseph. Father made Joseph a long robe with sleeves, something only the richest and most important Canaanites wore! Sometimes Joseph helped us with the sheep. But once he gave our father a bad report about us. Father believed what Joseph told him. Joseph always thought he was better than the rest of us! He used to boast about these fantastic dreams. In one dream there were twelve sheaves of grain in the field. All the other sheaves bowed down to his sheaf, which stood upright. Another time the stars, the moon, and the sun were all bowing down to him.

Reuben: I am Reuben, the oldest of the brothers. I am proud to be a good shepherd and a good son. But one day I made a terrible mistake. I deceived my father and caused him great grief.

Joseph was spoiled. He annoyed us with his boasting about special favors. One day when the rest of us were away from home tending the sheep, our father sent Joseph to see how we were. When my brothers saw him coming, they wanted to kill him. Who would ever know? But I said no, let's just put him in this deep pit. Then we will not be guilty of murder. I intended to come back later, pull Joseph from the pit, and send him back to our father.

But before I could return, my brothers sold Joseph to a passing caravan. We killed a goat, dipped Joseph's fine robe in the blood, and took it to our father. He thought that Joseph had been killed by a wild beast.

Joseph: I never knew my brothers hated me so much! I know now that I made a lot of mistakes. My father should not have favored me and my brother Benjamin. But our mother, Rachel, was his favorite wife. One day my father made me a wonderful robe with long sleeves. Such robes were worn by rich Canaanites, not by common shepherd boys. No wonder my brothers resented me!

I thought I would die in that pit. I was frightened and confused when my brothers hauled me out and sold me to a caravan on its way to Egypt. I prayed to the God of my father Jacob, and of Isaac, and of Abraham. God was surely with me, since I am now the slave of one of Pharaoh's officials, Potiphar. Potiphar has put me in charge of all his household and possessions. I am thankful that God has watched over me and has delivered me from all my fears.

Day 1

As you read today's Bible story with your children, pause at each point of thoughtlessness or cruelty, and discuss, "How might the lives of Jacob's family have been better if this character had chosen to act in a different way?"

Day 2

Make a simple crossword puzzle from the names of your family members. Then ask the children to provide clues such as "the one who makes delicious chocolate cake" or "the one who got an A on her spelling test." Help them think of positive affirming statements that will strengthen their appreciation of and bonding to each other.

Day 3

Select news stories from the daily paper that your children will understand. Talk about the ways bad situations may be used for good by God. Is there a way you (perhaps through your church or community) could help in any of these situations?

Day 4

Toss a blanket over a small table to make a tent for your younger children to play in. Encourage their imaginations as they pretend to live in the desert country of Canaan, care for the sheep, or ride the camels in a caravan. If you have Internet access, or can use the Internet in the library, let your older children look up living in tents today. (Hint: try the word *yurts*.)

Day 5

Recall a thoughtless word or action from a family member (start with the adults, please!). Help the person who was thoughtless to think of at least two things he or she could have said or done instead. Remember that a thinking climate assists in faith development!

Day 6

Make a Bible verse reminder for your meal table. You will need 4-by-6 cards, fine-line markers, a paper punch, and binder rings. Use one card as the cover. If you have children who cannot read or write, let them decorate the cover. Print one favorite Bible verse on each 4-by-6 card. Let family members use a variety of fine-line markers to make the cards colorful. Punch two holes in the top of each card. Be sure the holes are the same place on every card. Put all the cards, including the cover card, into the binder rings. Turn one card over each day or at each meal.

Day 7

Read this fable: Once there was a man with seven sons. The brothers quarreled all the time, giving their father no peace from their endless arguing. One day the father handed each son a stick. "See if you can break it!" he commanded. Each son took his stick and easily broke it. The father then took seven more sticks. These he bound into a secure bundle. He handed the bundle to the first son. The son struggled and groaned, but he could not break the bundle. All seven sons struggled to break the bundle, but not one to them could do it. "You see," commented the father, "it is easy to break one alone. But it is impossible to break seven who are bound to each other."

Joseph the Leader

Talk Point:

God was with Joseph in Egypt—in prison and when he became a ruler. God will be with us when we are in trouble and when other people are counting on our help.

God was with Joseph in the household of Potiphar in Egypt. Potiphar entrusted everything he had to Joseph.

Trouble came when Potiphar's wife wanted Joseph to do wrong. When Joseph refused, she told lies to Potiphar. Potiphar believed her. He had Joseph thrown into prison.

But even while Joseph was in prison, God continued to bless him. The chief jailer trusted Joseph and put all the prisoners in Joseph's care.

One day the cupbearer and the baker of the king of Egypt, who were also in prison, told Joseph about some disturbing dreams they had had. Joseph was able to tell them what the dreams meant. The cupbearer, Joseph said, would soon be restored to his position with the pharaoh. When the cupbearer rejoiced, Joseph said, "Remember me. Mention me to Pharaoh and get me out of this place."

It was two whole years before the cupbearer thought of Joseph. But when the pharaoh had a strange dream that no one could interpret, the cupbearer remembered Joseph.

Pharaoh sent for Joseph. "In my dream seven fat, sleek cows were eaten up by seven ugly and thin cows. In a second dream seven ears of grain, full and good, were eaten up by seven withered, blighted ears."

Joseph said, "God sent the dreams to tell you that there will be seven years of plenty and prosperity in Egypt. But these years will be followed by seven years of drought. Pharaoh should appoint a wise man to prepare. Let the people store one-fifth of the grain in the good years to keep the people from starvation during the bad years."

Everything happened as Pharaoh had dreamed. During the seven good years Joseph directed the storage of grain in every city. Soon all the storehouses were bulging.

At the end of seven years a famine came upon the land. When the Egyptians had eaten all they had, they came to the pharaoh asking for food. Pharaoh told them to go to Joseph. Joseph opened the storehouses and sold the grain so that the people would not starve. People from other countries came to Egypt to buy grain too.

Joseph, who had arrived in Egypt as a slave, had been used by God to bring good to the whole world.

Day 1 Talk about leadership qualities. Give everyone a piece of paper and lay out markers. Ask your family to think about the qualities of a leader. (Some qualities you may name are friendly, caring, wise, obedient, respectful of others, neat, and unafraid.) Help family members see their own good qualities. Younger children may draw pictures; older people may list words and draw pictures as well. Title your pages "Leader" and put them in your "Wondrous Things" scrapbook.

Day 2 Make simple table prayer cards by folding construction paper so it will stand up. On one side have your child print Psalm 25:4-5. Let other family members decorate the other side. Use this verse as a prayer before meals this week.

Day 3 Draw or cut out from wallpaper or brown paper a rough outline of the place you live. Have all the members of your family find pictures in old magazines that illustrate a time when God is with your family. Overlap and glue these on the outline to make a montage that you can display. Spray the montage with non-aerosol hair spray. The title of your montage could be "God is With Us."

Day 4 Use old newspapers and a piece of construction paper. Cut out pictures, news items, or words that show leadership—either good or bad. Overlap and glue the items at different angles so that no space is seen on your paper. Use a marker to write "What Kind of Leadership Does God Bless?" as a title at the top. When it is dry, add it to your "Wondrous Things" scrapbook. Talk about what made Joseph a special, good leader.

Day 5 Read Genesis 40 and 41. Write a news article about Joseph. For a real scoop, read Genesis 41:34-35. It doesn't sound like Pharaoh paid for the grain that was taken from the farmers. How might the people have reacted to this decision? Your children might prefer to present this as a TV news story.

Day 6 Once Joseph dreamed that the stars bowed down to him. Cut out seven star shapes. Using Genesis 40 and 41, write one leadership trait that you see in Joseph on each star. Cut out a star for each family member. Write a leadership trait on each person's star. Make a mobile to hang over your table.

Day 7 Children are always eager to know "the rest of the story." Nurture a sense of anticipation for hearing next week's story. Ask: "What do you think Joseph's brothers were doing all this time? Do you think his father was still grieving for him? Do you think Benjamin missed Joseph? Do you think Jacob made Benjamin his favorite after Joseph disappeared?"

Joseph Forgave

Scripture:
Genesis 42:1-2, 29-36;
43:1-17, 23; 44:1-13,
18, 33-34; 45:1-5
Psalm 72:12

Talk Point:
Joseph forgave his brothers and told them that God had worked through him to feed the hungry. God can work through people today to help those in need.

When the famine reached Canaan, Jacob sent his sons to buy grain in Egypt. Benjamin remained at home with Jacob, for Jacob feared that harm might come to his youngest son.

When the brothers bowed before the governor of Egypt, they did not recognize him as their brother Joseph. But Joseph knew his brothers immediately. Their answers to his many questions assured Joseph that his father and his brother Benjamin were alive and well.

Joseph wanted to ensure that his brothers would return to Egypt. "Take this food to your hungry households," he said. "but Simeon must remain here until you return with your youngest brother."

When the brothers told their father Jacob of the governor's actions, Jacob would not allow Benjamin to go to Egypt. "I have lost Joseph and now Simeon!" he mourned. "I will not let Benjamin be lost to me also."

But when the grain was all eaten, there was nothing else to do. Jacob allowed the brothers to take Benjamin with them to Egypt. Joseph ordered his servant to prepare a special meal. Simeon was returned to his brothers, and everyone feasted.

Joseph tested his brothers. He had a servant put his silver cup in Benjamin's sack of grain. When the brothers had traveled a little way, a servant was sent to ask them, "Why have you stolen the governor's silver cup?" Of course the cup was found in Benjamin's sack. All the brothers returned to the city to plead for Benjamin.

Joseph told them that Benjamin must remain as his slave. What despair the brothers felt! Judah pleaded with Joseph, "This will kill our father. He has already lost one son. Allow me to stay as your slave. Let the boy return to our father."

Joseph could stand it no longer. He sent all the Egyptians away. He began to weep. He told his brothers that he was the one they had sold into slavery. "Do not be distressed," he said. "God sent me here to preserve life. Because I am here, many people will survive the famine, and your families will be saved." Joseph and his brothers wept together. The brothers saw that Joseph had forgiven them, and they trusted God.

Day 1

Roleplay the scene where Joseph reveals that he is their brother. Let family members choose one of the brothers to roleplay. (Persons to suggest might be Reuben, Simeon, Judah, Dan, Joseph, and Benjamin.) Suggest that each player think of one sentence that the brother he or she has chosen might be thinking. Have a good time! Then remind the players that Joseph was not perfect. However, God still chose him. God worked through Joseph to bring good to the Hebrew people as well as to the Egyptians. Joseph was able to forgive his brothers because he could see God's hand in bringing good to every circumstance in life.

Day 2

Challenge family members to make up a code. Use symbols, musical notes, stars, or whatever you can think of to replace the alphabet. Then write a simple Bible verse in code and give it to other family members to solve. Younger children can work with parents. If you choose the verse, "God is love," you will only need to come up with eight symbols. Perhaps you would like to send copies of the codes to friends or family members who live far away.

Day 3

Remind your family that all of the stories you have been reading are about people who were Abraham's descendants. God made a promise to Abraham. Let everyone make a banner for his or her bedroom with the phrase, "God Keeps Promises." Provide paper, glue, and glitter. Talk about the meaning of the phrase as you work.

Day 4

This would be a good time to take a nighttime walk. Try to count the stars! Do you think Abraham's descendants are as many as the stars? Give thanks for families.

Day 5

Reread Genesis 43:11. Take a trip to the grocery store and buy pistachio nuts and almonds. Enjoy a Holy Land snack. (If you buy the pistachios in the shell, children will enjoy shelling them as they eat.) Thank God for favorite foods.

Day 6

Make a list of some of the characters in the stories you have been reading. Almost all of them made mistakes! Ask family members to recall the mistakes and how God used the mistakes for good.

Day 7

Make lentil soup and deliver it to another family or to a shelter for the homeless.

Baby in a Basket

Miriam held her baby brother in her lap as she watched her mother working busily on a basket. Miriam tickled the baby's fat chin with a bit of grass until he laughed.

Jochebed made sure that the basket was tightly woven of the tall grasses that grew at the edge of the Nile River. Then she spread natural tar all over the basket. As she worked, Jochebed gently answered her daughter's questions.

"Pharaoh is angry at the midwives," she explained softly. "He is afraid that there are too many Hebrews in Egypt. He needs us to build his cities; but he is afraid that if there are too many of us, he would not be able to stop us from leaving Egypt. So he commanded Shiphrah and Puah to kill all of our baby boys as soon as they are born."

"But our baby is safe, isn't he, Mother?" asked Miriam.

"Shiphrah and Puah have done a brave thing," said Jochebed. "They have not killed the babies. They told Pharaoh that the Hebrew women are strong. They told him that our babies came so quickly, they could not get there in time to kill the babies."

Miriam was thoughtful. "What will Pharaoh do now?"

"He has commanded that all Hebrew baby boys be thrown into the Nile."

"Oh, Mother, what will we do?" wailed Miriam.

"Follow me," said Mother. Quickly and quietly they found their way to the edge of the Nile River.

Jochebed put the finished basket carefully among the reeds in the river. The basket was secure and dry. She lifted the baby lovingly from Miriam's arms and put him in the basket.

"Watch here," she said to Miriam. "Do not be frightened. God will take care of our baby."

In a little while the daughter of Pharaoh came to the river to bathe. She lifted Moses out of the basket and said that she would adopt him as her own son. When Miriam saw the princess had found the baby, she was very brave. "Shall I get a nurse for the baby?" she asked. And Miriam brought her mother to Pharaoh's daughter to care for Moses.

Day 1 Read Isaiah 41:10a. Talk about God's promise in this verse. Tell your child about personal experiences of God's presence with you.

Day 2 Use strips of paper to weave place mats. As you weave, talk about how Moses' family must have felt as Jochebed prepared the tiny cradle-boat for her baby.

Day 3 Make a list of courageous women you and your family know today. Can you think of women in government? working with persons who are homeless and hungry? working through the church? as homemakers? in the media? Talk about how their acts of courage compare with the midwives in the story of Moses.

Day 4 Talk about the courageous children in the Bible story. Miriam and Moses were raised to know that God was with them. In what situations might your children need to call upon God for courage? Talk about those times with your family. Thank God for Bible stories that tell us about the love and care of God.

Day 5 Take a trip to the library to find books about women of courage. Some names to look for are Harriet Stubbs, Corrie ten Boom, and Rosa Parks. Look for books about other biblical women as well, such as Esther and Deborah.

Day 6 This would be a good time to play with play dough. Encourage children to make baby Moses and his basket. As you work, talk about the preparations you made while you were waiting for your children to be born or adopted. Thank God for families.

Day 7 Enjoy the video, "Moses, Prince of Egypt," as a family. Is there a lonely child in your neighborhood you could invite to join you?

Play Dough

1 cup flour
1/3 cup salt
1/3 to 1/2 cup water
few drops of cooking oil
few drops of food coloring.

Mix the flour and salt in a bowl. Add the water and oil slowly.
Knead the dough until it is the consistency you want. (Add a little more flour and salt if the mixture is too sticky.)
Add drops of food coloring and continue to knead the dough until it is the color you want it to be. Keep the play dough at room temperature in an airtight container.

Trouble for Moses

Scripture:
Exodus 2:11-21
Psalm 56:3-4

Talk Point:

Moses acted without God's guidance, then ran away. God was with Moses, even when he did what was wrong. God will always be with us.

A Might-have-been Play

Characters
Hebrew man beaten by an Egyptian
Hebrew wife
Hebrew friend

Scene: Inside a Hebrew home in Egypt

Hebrew man: I would not be alive today if it weren't for Moses! O-o-o-h, how I ache from that beating!

Friend: Hush, not so loud. You don't want the Egyptians to hear you. That might mean another beating, you know.

Wife: Thank God you are alive, but when will we ever see Moses again? He should not have killed that Egyptian.

Friend: I think Moses was caught by surprise. I think when he saw that Egyptian beating you, he just lost his temper. Moses is a fine young man and loyal to the Hebrew people, but he has a lot to learn.

Hebrew man: Yes, he committed a great sin. I wish he had stopped to pray and ask God for guidance. Perhaps if he had done that, he would still be here with us.

Wife: I wish we knew where to find Moses. He fled so fast that no one knows when he is. Do you think he's still alive?

Friend: We believe so, but even Pharaoh's daughter, who raised Moses as her own son, cannot protect him now that he has killed an Egyptian. Moses had to run away. But God will watch over him.

Wife: I remember the basket that his mother made when Pharaoh commanded that our baby boys be killed. God surely watched over Moses then!

Hebrew man: God must have a great purpose for Moses. We must comfort his mother, sister, and brother until Moses returns. I will never forget that Moses saved my life.

Day 1   Read the story from the Bible in Exodus 2:11-21 either before or after you read the play. Can you explain how God would protect and watch over someone who has done wrong?

Day 2   Make characters from the story by using round-head clothespins, chenille stems, and fabric scraps. Draw facial features at the top of the clothespins. Wrap a piece of chenille stem around the clothespin to create arms. Use fabric scraps to make clothes for the figures. Glue the clothes to the clothespins or tie them on with a strip of cloth. Use yarn to make hair and beards. Stand your figures in a clump of clay.

Day 3   Talk about conflicts in your family. Recall a recent conflict and give everyone a chance to suggest solutions. Help family members learn to deal with conflict by talking to God about a solution. Write a short prayer that could be used anytime a family member needs help.

Day 4   Go from "Hate" to "Love" in four steps.

H A T E
_ A T E
_ A _ E
_ _ _ E
L O V E

Can you make up other brain teasers? Try "Kill" to "Save."

Day 5   Life was hard for the Hebrews in Egypt. Read these verses in Exodus 5 to discover some of the things that happened to the Hebrews while they were Pharaoh's slaves: verses 7, 9, 14, 15, 16, 18, and 23.

Day 6   Look up the history of brick making on the Internet or in an encyclopedia. Thank God for the wonders of creation that enable human beings to make building materials.

Day 7   In the United States slaves made the bricks that were used to construct Jamestown, Virginia. Talk with your family about the blot slavery has made on God's world almost from the beginning of time. Thank God for people who were willing to stand up and say that it is never all right for one person to own another.

The Burning Bush

Scripture:
Exodus 3:1-14; 4:1, 10-17
Psalm 119:105

Talk Point:
God called Moses to help the people of Israel and promised to be with Moses. God calls us to help others and promises to be with us.

Have you ever been told to do something that you didn't want to do? That happened one day to Moses. He had lived for many years with Jethro. He had married Jethro's daughter, Zipporah, and had children. He tended to Jethro's sheep. He was content and happy.

One day when Moses had taken the sheep a long way from home to find grass, he saw a strange sight. A bush seemed to be on fire, yet Moses could see that the bush was not burning up. *I never saw anything like that before,* Moses thought. *I must go over there to see this curious bush.*

Then God called to Moses from the bush. "Moses, Moses!"

Moses answered right away, "Here I am!"

God said to Moses, "Don't come any closer! You must take your sandals off because the ground under your feet is holy."

When Moses realized that it was God speaking to him, he hid his face. He was afraid to look at God.

God told Moses that the Israelites were still suffering in Egypt. God's plan was to save the people from all their troubles in Egypt and to bring them to the wonderful land of Canaan.

"So come on!" said God. "You must go to Pharaoh and bring all my people out of Egypt."

Moses was not happy with what he was hearing. He did not want to go to the pharaoh! He did not want to leave Midian! He did not feel that he was the right person for the job.

Moses began to make excuses. "The people won't believe me," he said. "They will not listen to me. They will not think I am a good leader. Oh, please send someone else!"

God was provoked with Moses. "I will send your brother Aaron to help you," he promised. "I will be with you."

Then Moses knew that he must do what God commanded. He took the staff that God would use to help him. He was willing to answer God's call to help his people.

Day 1 Talk about Moses and Aaron. God expects brothers and sisters to help one another. Moses relied on his brother Aaron and and his sister Miriam. Encourage your family to make a list of ways they can help one another. Check at the end of each day to add to the list or to praise children for their helpfulness.

Day 2 Make a frieze to display along one wall. A frieze is a border of pictures that can be used to tell a story to illustrate an idea. Let family members draw around their hands and then cut out the handprints. Look through magazines and find small pictures of people being helpful. Glue the pictures to the handprints. Roll out a strip of butcher paper as long as the area where you will place the display. Glue your handprints onto the strip and then hang the strip on the wall.

Day 3 Think about Moses and the Midianites. Thousands of years ago the people of Israel and the rest of the Middle East were brothers and cousins. Find Egypt, Canaan, and Midian on a Bible-times map (there is probably a map in your Bible, if you do not have another). Do you remember the relationship of these important areas? Find a news story about the Middle East today. Pray for peace in the Middle East and in the whole world.

Day 4 Read Psalm 119:105. Ask family members to write the meaning of the verse in their own words. A good modern day illustration for *lamp* and *light* is a flashlight. Turn off all the lights in the house and find your way from one room to another without any light. Then use a flashlight to light the way. Thank God for the Bible, which helps us to see the way God wants us to go.

Day 5 Think together as a family about ways your family can be helpful to another family. (Could you babysit for a young couple? offer to drive another family to worship and to Sunday school? assemble a kit of personal items for a family living in a shelter?) Plan how you will carry out your idea.

Day 6 Plan a family games night. Let everyone suggest a game. The rule is that every game is played at least once (you may need more than one night). Older children may complain about younger siblings' choices, but they will be surprised how much fun they can have if they really enter into the spirit of play. Be sure to thank the children for their suggestions and to praise them for playing together as a family.

Day 7 Trade chores. Let younger children try more difficult chores while the older children get a break with easy chores. Thank God for God's play for families.

Moses Obeys God

Scripture:
Exodus 4:20—5:9,
22-23; 6:1;
7:14—12:32, 41

Talk Point:
Moses obeyed God's call, and God worked through Moses to lead the people of Israel to freedom. When we obey God, God can work through us.

(One reader reads the Leader parts; family responds with "Let my people go!")

Leader: Moses and Aaron went to Pharaoh and asked that the Israelites be permitted to leave Egypt to worship God. But Pharaoh responded by making the work of the slaves even harder than before. Finally God told Moses, "Now you shall see what I will do to Pharaoh" . . . And as the LORD commanded, Moses and Aaron struck the waters of the Nile and all the water . . . turned into blood" (Exodus 6:1; 7:20).

Family: Let my people go!

Leader: But Pharaoh would not let the people go. According to the Lord's command, "frogs came up and covered the land of Egypt" (8:6).

Family: Let my people go!

Leader: But Pharaoh would not let the people go. Aaron struck the dust of the earth, and it turned into gnats.

Family: Let my people go!

Leader: "Great swarms of flies came . . . the land was ruined" (8:24).

Family: Let my people go!

Leader: All the livestock of the Egyptians died.

Family: Let my people go!

Leader: Moses took soot . . . and threw it in the air, and it caused boils.

Family: Let my people go!

Leader: "And the LORD rained hail on the land of Egypt" (9:23).

Family: Let my people go!

Leader: "Locusts came upon all the land of Egypt" (10:14-15).

Family: Let my people go!

Leader: "So Moses stretched out his hand toward heaven, and there was dense darkness in all the land . . . for three days" (10:22).

Family: Let my people go!

Leader: At midnight the Lord struck down all the firstborn in the land of Egypt. Then at last Pharaoh said, "Take your flocks and your herds and be gone!"

Day 1 Have fun reading the Bible story and then read it from the Bible as well (you may want to choose a children's Bible).

Day 2 Reread these verses from Exodus 11:2; 12:34, 35, and 38. The Israelites did not have much time to get ready to move! Let each family member choose something he or she would do if the family was getting ready to move (packing clothes, packing toys or other items, taking a bath or shower, packing food to eat on the journey). Act out the choices and let other family members try to guess what you are doing. Then ask: "Did the Israelites have time for this?"

Day 3 Do your family members make excuses instead of owning up to shortcomings and letting the whole family help? Set a good example for your children. Don't let them learn the habit of excuse making from you! For one week write down every time a family member makes an excuse. Deal immediately with the issue. Instead of agreeing with "I didn't bring in my bicycle because it was raining," help your child to say, "I should have brought my bicycle in. Now I will have to wax it." Let the children remind you when you need to stop making excuses too! Thank God for families who help.

Day 4 Get a recording of "Go Down, Moses" and sing it together. Can you write other verses? If so, write them down for your "Wondrous Things" scrapbook.

Day 5 Take a trip to the library and get a book about Harriett Tubman, who has been referred to as the "Black Moses." Read the book together. Why do we call her that? Can you think of any people today who are answering God's call to help others? Say a special prayer for them. Does your church support a missionary? Send him or her a card of thanks for answering God's call.

Day 6 Encourage family members to draw or write their own version of this week's story to add to your "Wondrous Things" scrapbook.

Day 7 When the Israelites left, many Egyptians gave them jewelry to take along. Use gold spray paint to paint pasta and then string on nylon cord to make necklaces and bracelets like the Egyptians might have worn.

Free At Last

Talk Point:
Through Moses, God led the people of Israel when they faced danger and were afraid. We can trust God when we are troubled and afraid.

Anchor: Good morning! This is Radio Station OUT, the morning news center of Goshen. Today there is a mass gathering of the Israelite slaves near the Red Sea. The authorities fully expected these people to take the trade route out of Egypt, but instead they have taken the Wilderness Road. We have reports that their God led them in a pillar of cloud by day and in a pillar of fire at night. Our reporter, Micah, is on the scene to bring you the latest development in the uprising of the slaves. Micah, what's happening there?

Reporter (very excited)**:** This is a scene we will never forget! The impossible is happening! Pharaoh's chariots and his finest troops are chasing the Israelites into the sea! Moses led all these people along the Wilderness Road. They camped beside the sea. When they saw that they were being pursued by the Egyptian troops, they were very frightened. There was no place to go! Ahead was the sea, and behind were the troops of Egypt. It looked as though the slaves would be turned like a herd of cattle and sent back to Egypt to make bricks. It was an impossible situation!

Anchor: Wait, Micah. You said the troops were chasing the people into the sea. Surely they will drown!

Reporter: Not at all! This I cannot understand! As the people drew near the sea, with the chariots coming swiftly behind them, Moses lifted his staff. An east wind, even mightier than the strongest wind we have seen before, began to blow. We were terrified! But the wind blew the sea aside. The slaves were able to walk on dry ground to the other side. Even their animals, their children, and their oldest folks went into that sea path!

Anchor: This is astonishing. But won't the chariots just follow them to the other side of the sea? The Israelites cannot possibly get away from Pharaoh's army.

Reporter: No, no! I can hardly believe what I am seeing! Their God is mighty indeed! The sea is closing in! The sea is closing in! (*pause*) The chariots of Pharaoh are gone! From this side we can see the Israelite people. The are awed at what God has done. No wonder these people listen to Moses!

Day 1 Children today live in a frightening time. Help them to understand that God will always be with them. Be sure, however, that they know that they must do their own part by being careful and safe. Roleplay various situations that a child may be in. Talk about the best way to handle each situation.

Day 2 Play "Follow the Leader." Talk with your children about who they can trust as people they should follow.

Day 3 Tell your child about a time in your life when you especially experienced God's presence. Did you feel less afraid or worried? How can your child learn to know that God is always present?

Day 4 Talk with your family about miracles. Any time we read about God's miracles in the Bible, children may be stimulated to ask, "Why doesn't God do that today?" Help your child understand the answers you would give to that question. If you are comfortable with the concept, you might check out some books about modern-day miracles.

Day 5 Provide family members with new note pads. Encourage each member to draw successive small pictures of the Exodus in the right-hand corner. As the corner is rapidly flipped, the drawings seem to move. Presto, the Exodus!

Day 6 Take a trip to the library to find books with maps of Bible lands. Enjoy looking through the books. Because of our lack of knowledge about the geography of the area, no one knows for sure exactly what route the Israelites took when they left Egypt. Today we do not know where the towns mentioned in Exodus 14:2 were located. Early translators translated the name of the sea near which the Israelites camped as the Red Sea. However, a more accurate translation of the original Hebrew word are the words *sea* and *reeds*. Reeds did not grow around the Red Sea, but they did grow near Lake Timsah. So we are not sure exactly where the miracle of the crossing of the sea took place. However, it is important to remember that God made it possible.

Day 7 If your Bible or one of the books you checked out has a map of the Exodus, look carefully at the map. Do you see:
* the trade route that God decided not to use?
* the possible route of the Exodus?
* the Gulf of Suez?
* Lake Timsah?
* Mount Sinai (or Horeb)?
* the land of Midian?
* the land of Canaan?

In the Wilderness

Talk Point:
God provided for the people of Israel when they needed food and water in the wilderness. We can trust God to care about us and our needs.

After God's great miracle at the Red Sea, the Israelites went into the desert. After three days the people began to complain, "What are we to drink? This water is bitter!" God told Moses to throw a piece of wood into the water. When he did, the water became sweet. The Israelites and their livestock drank their fill.

Soon the Israelites had eaten all the bread they had brought out of Egypt. They began to complain again. "We should have stayed in Egypt where we had plenty to eat. Why did Moses bring us out here where we will all die of hunger?"

God heard the complaining and told Moses and Aaron to speak to the people. In the evening God would send meat to eat. And in the morning God would send bread. God would provide for the people.

That evening quails came up and covered the camp. The Israelites had plenty of meat. In the morning when the dew dried, everything was covered with a fine flaky substance. "What is it?" asked the people. "God has sent bread," said Moses and Aaron. "Each morning gather as much as you need for your family. Do not be greedy and gather more! But on the sixth day of the week, you must gather enough for two days. God will not send manna on the sabbath, for the sabbath is a day of rest. On that day you will eat the manna that you gathered the previous day."

The manna tasted like crackers made with honey, and the people had food to eat. But some people did not listen. They gathered more than enough manna. By the next day, it had become wormy and was no good at all. However, on the sixth day the manna did not spoil, for God intended it for food for the people on the sabbath.

Once again water became difficult to find in the desert. The people complained again.

"What can I do?" Moses asked God. "The people are angry. They may stone me!" God reminded Moses of his marvelous staff, the same one that he held up at the Red Sea. God told Moses to strike a rock with the staff. When Moses obeyed God, water rushed out from the rock, and everyone had plenty to drink.

Sometimes the Israelite people forgot God's promise to take care of them. Sometimes they forgot their part of the covenant too. But while they were in the wilderness, they were reminded that God would provide for them.

Day 1 — There are some days when a child is cranky and whines about everything. Often it is because the child is hungry, thirsty, uncomfortable, sick, or troubled. Search first for such causes. However, if the crankiness is pure habit, ask your child (not yourself!) to record each time he or she whines or complains. At the end of each day talk about the list. Decide together what your child can do to become a happier person. Offer encouragement and praise.

Day 2 — What about the adults in your family? Are you ever cranky? Make a list of the elements in your life that usually cause you to complain. Let your children help you write a prayer that you can use to deal with these problems. Thank God for families who help one another.

Day 3 — Memorize Psalm 46:1 together. Put each word on a card. Mix up the cards. Then make a game of putting the verse together correctly.

Day 4 — Talk with your child about the times when God has provided for you when you thought there was noplace to turn to for help. Are there times when your child has felt that way? Thank God for caring for us.

Day 5 — Enjoy manna:

Manna

one package filo dough, unthawed
1/3 stick butter
1/3 cup honey
3 tablespoon sugar
1 teaspoon ground coriander (optional)
non-stick cooking spray.

Filo dough may be found with frozen pie crusts in the freezer case. This recipe is based on 9-by-14-inch pastry leaves (package contains 40 leaves) but varying sizes of filo dough will work.

Preheat oven to 400 degrees. Melt butter with honey. Stir in sugar and coriander.

To begin the layering process, coat a baking sheet with non-stick spray and place one filo leaf on the sheet. Work quickly as leaves dry out. Brush with the butter mixture, then place another leaf on top. Repeat until 8 layers have been brushed.

Bake in the oven for five minutes or until golden and just browning on the edges. Remove from the oven and immediately cut into pieces. Serves ten.

Day 6 — Draw with sidewalk chalk. Talk about how Moses' staff was a symbol of God's power. Think of symbols you have seen in church or in pictures in Bible storybooks. Draw symbols on the sidewalk with chalk. (Hint: If you dip the chalk in water first, you will have brighter colors!)

Day 7 — Talk about the stories of God's people that you have read so far. Let each person share something from his or her favorite story. Say a thank you prayer for the person in the story after each person has shared (for example: "Thank you, God, for Moses").

God's Law

Moses and the Israelites had been traveling in the desert for three months. One day they came to the wilderness of Sinai. They could see a fine plain at the foot of Mount Sinai. Moses told the people to make camp there. Moses knew that they were at the holy mountain of God. He was not surprised when God called to him from the mountain.

Moses went up on the mountain, where God told him that the people must obey God's voice and keep the covenant. God told Moses that the people must wash their clothes and prepare themselves to hear God in three days.

All the Israelites washed their clothes. They did exactly as Moses said to do. They did not know what to expect. Many of them were frightened.

On the third day the mountain seemed to be on fire. There was a cloud of smoke. The mountain shook and trembled. There was thunder and lightning and the blare of a trumpet.

While Moses was on the mountain, God spoke the words of the Ten Commandments.

God said that the people must worship only God.

God said that no one should make an image of gold or silver to worship, nor should they worship any god but God.

God said that God's name must not be used inappropriately.

God also said that the sabbath day should be kept holy. People must remember that this is a day of rest and worship. God rested after the work of Creation, and God sets the sabbath aside for people to rest.

These were the first four of the Ten Commandments. They helped the people know how they should obey God.

Then God gave Moses six more commandments. These commandments would help people know how to treat one another.

God said: Honor your parents.
       Do not murder.
       Be faithful in marriage.
       Do not steal.
       Do not lie.
       Do not covet what others have.

Day 1   As you travel to and from school, the store, and church with your family this week, notice different safety signs such as stop signs, yield signs, entrance and exit signs, and so forth. Together decide how those signs are for your benefit and protection. Explain that God's Word also has rules for our benefit and protection.

Day 2   Every family has rules. Help your family list the rules your family observes. Discuss the reason for each rule. Is it to keep family members safe? healthy? Is it to ensure that family members and others are treated with respect?

Day 3   If you have preschool or younger elementary-age children, make an "I Can Obey" chart. Together list the rules your child has to follow at home. (Examples: Go to Sunday school and church on Sunday. Brush my teeth. Be kind to my brother or sister. Go to bed without whining.) List the days of the week across the top of the chart. Purchase colorful stickers. Each time your child obeys, put the sticker in the appropriate space. Praise your child for his or her obedience. Help your child understand that when everyone follows the rules, you have a happier family.

Day 4   Encourage older children to make a word scramble using Leviticus 19:18b. Work together to unscramble the words and to memorize the verse.

Day 5   Make clay tablets of the first commandment. Give each person clay (or homemade play dough) and a craft stick or dull pencil. Flatten out the clay and round off the tops to look like stone tablets. Use the craft stick or pencil to write the first commandment on the clay. As you work, remember that this and the next three commandments tell us ways that we can obey God. Is there someone who would enjoy receiving one of the tablets?

Day 6   Jesus talked about commandments too. Read Matthew 22:35-40. Are these two commandments new? Or do they really say the same thing the Ten Commandments say? What verses of Exodus 20 are similar to Jesus' first commandments? What verses of Exodus 20 are part of Jesus' second commandment? Thank God for Jesus, who came to show us how to live as God wants us to live.

Day 7   In addition to the Ten Commandments, there are hundreds of other rules recorded in the Pentateuch. Read these rules that the Hebrew people used to measure how they were doing in their relationships to one another. Then suggest one word or a phrase that describes what each rule is about: Leviticus 19:9-10; Leviticus 25:35-37; Numbers 15:37-40; and Deuteronomy 26:1-15. Are any of these rules that we keep today?

Crossing the Jordan

Scripture:
Joshua 1:10-11;
3:1—4:7; 24:14-17, 24

Talk Point:
Joshua was able to lead the people of Israel because he listened to God an obeyed God. We can listen to God and let God work through us.

Although Moses had served God faithfully for many years, he did not lead the people of Israel into Canaan. Joshua was chosen to be the new leader. Moses told him to be strong and courageous. Joshua knew that God would not leave the Israelites. He knew that we can trust God to keep promises.

Joshua strode through the camp talking to the officers of the people. "Tell everyone to prepare provisions! In three days we will cross over the Jordan and take possession of the land God has given us!"

All the people were excited. God had made Joshua their new leader. Across the river they could see the lush grass and the hills that loomed over the valley. This was to be their land, their new home! It was almost too good to be true.

But how will we get across the river? some of them must have wondered. There were old people and babies. There were thousands of sheep and donkeys and camels and goats. The river was at flood stage. This was not going to be easy.

After three days Joshua gave instructions. He told the priests to carry the Ark of the Covenant into the river and to stand there. The ark contained the Ten Commandments as well as some manna. It was a very holy box.

When the priests all stood with their feet in the water, God caused the waters of the river to pile up above that place. Then all the people crossed over the Jordan River. The priests stood on dry ground while the people were crossing.

Joshua did not want the people to forget this miracle of God. He said to the people, "Choose twelve men, one from each tribe. The twelve men must take twelve stones from the riverbed and carry them on their shoulders to the place where we will camp. There we will make a memorial of the stones. When your children someday ask, 'What is that pile of stones?' you will tell them of this great day when the Lord took you across the Jordan on dry land."

Joshua led the people for many years. They won the land from their enemies. Joshua often reminded them that it was God who fought for them. He told the people to worship and to serve God. The people knew that Joshua was strong and courageous and wise. They promised to serve God.

Day 1   Decide together on leadership tasks for each family member. Be sure that the tasks assigned to children reflect each child's talent or ability. Someone may plan meals, lead in family prayers, choose games for Family Fun Night, or purchase or plan for mission gifts. At the end of a week, evaluate as a family to see if members have grown in their ability to take leadership.

Day 2   Put the words *Strong* and *Courageous* on a bulletin board or on the refrigerator door. Whenever anyone in the family exhibits those characteristics, recognize it and write that person's name under the words.

Day 3   Pray for the leadership in your community, your congregation, and your country. Write a letter of appreciation and encouragement to someone either in your church or your community. Go as a family to mail the letter, admiring the wonder of your own "land" on the way.

Day 4   Beginning with Joshua the Bible includes books of history. These twelve Old Testament books tell us about parts of the early history of Israel. Look at the table of contents in your Bible with your family. List the twelve books from Joshua to Esther. Write the title "Books of History" across the top of the page and then decorate the page. Add the pages to your "Wondrous Things" scrapbook.

Day 5   Find smooth stones or cut out paper stones. Write on the stones the name of a "hallowed" or special person who has helped the family in some way, particularly in ways of knowing and understanding God.

Day 6   If your family chose a praise chorus or wrote a family cheer earlier in the year, sing or shout it now. Remember that we are all part of God's family. If you have not yet done so, work on a family cheer.

Day 7   Take a drive or walk through your town (or a nearby town). What visual reminders do you see—statues, buildings, parks, streets, and so on—that help you to remember what certain people have done?

Deborah

Talk Point:
God sent judges such
as Deborah to help the
Israelites obey God and
overcome their
enemies. We can obey
God and help others to
obey and serve.

The Israelites listened to Joshua and worshiped God as long as Joshua was alive. But when Joshua and the other leaders who had seen what God had done in the wilderness died, the people began to listen to their pagan neighbors. Most of them forgot about God. The Israelites became weak. Soon their enemies were able to conquer them and make slaves of them in their own land.

Those who remembered God began to moan to God about their hardships. God sent them judges to help them. The judges helped to settle quarrels or decide punishment for crime. Some judges were military leaders. All of the judges were religious leaders sent by God.

Once when the people had been wicked, God sent Deborah as judge over all of Israel. Deborah often sat under a palm tree in the hill country. All of Israel came to her to settle their disputes and to receive advice.

One day Deborah called Barak (BAR-ak), a military leader of the Israelites. "The Lord commands you. Take ten thousand men and go to the Wadi Kishon (WA-de KIGH-shon)," she said. (A wadi is a deep ravine or riverbed through which water may rush during a flood.) "At the wadi you will meet the Canaanites and defeat them."

Barak must have wondered, *How can our army defeat the Canaanites? They have nine hundred chariots of iron and many warriors besides!*

But Barak answered, "I will go, if you will go with me. If you do not go with me, I will not go."

Deborah agreed. She went with Barak to summon their warriors to go to the wadi.

When Sisera (SIS-uh-ruh), the Canaanite general, heard about this uprising of the Israelite troops, he called his nine hundred chariots of iron and all his soldiers to fight. Deborah told Barak and the soldiers, "Up! This is the day! God will go with you and give you the victory!"

When Sisera's army saw the ten thousand Israelites, they panicked. Many of them fled on foot. Sisera's iron chariots did not do any good at all. God gave a great victory to Deborah and Barak and the Israelite fighters. Now the Israelites could live in peace for many years with Deborah as their judge.

Day 1 Talk with your family about Deborah. Encourage both your sons and daughters to value leadership in female and male alike. Note that Deborah was a married woman who lived in the hill country with her husband. Domesticity did not prevent Deborah from exercising her natural God-given role of judge. Look back through your "Wondrous Things" scrapbook and see how many of the leadership qualities that you have listed apply to Deborah.

Day 2 Say Psalm 146:2 with your family each day this week. Talk about what it means to praise God by the way we make decisions each day of our lives.

Day 3 Make sock puppets and act out the conversation between Deborah and Barak. Then think of a dispute that might arise in your family. Take turns being Deborah and let "her" give advice. (Yes, responsible adults remain the ultimate judges, but often a child can learn from looking at both sides of a dispute.)

Day 4 Make hand reminders. Give family members two sheets of construction paper each and let them draw around both their hands. Write on the fingers of the right hand outline things you have done to disobey God's rules. Write on the left hand what you did to correct the disobedient action and to better live by God's rules (for example, talked back to Mom, apologized to Mom).

Day 5 Do you and your family know of modern women whom God has blessed in positions of leadership? Can you name women who serve in education, medicine, agriculture, government, church, and other leadership roles? Write a letter to one of these women thanking her for her leadership.

Day 6 Make and wear a button that says thank you to God! Cut out a cardboard circle that will fit into a milk or juice cap. Lay the circle aside. Now cut out a circle from a self-adhesive label that will stick to the top of the bottle cap. On the sticky label write your words of thanks to God with a fine-line marker; pull the backing off and apply the label to the bottle cap. Position the bottle cap on a T-shirt or on the collar of another shirt. Reach in between the front and back of the T-shirt. With the shirt between your cardboard circle and the bottle cap, press the cardboard circle into the cap. This will hold the button in place.

Day 7 Write a family praise litany using Psalm 146:2 as the response. Let each person think of one thing for which he or she is thankful and say it out loud. The rest of the family responds with, "I will praise the LORD as long as I live. I will sing praises to my God all my life long."

I Will Go With You!

Scripture:
Ruth 1:1-22

Talk Point:
God was with Ruth when she left her home to care for Naomi. We can know God's love through the love we receive and the love we share.

It was a difficult time. Naomi was very sad, but crying would not change things. She must make a decision. Years ago her family had traveled to Moab to survive a famine in Judah. In Moab her sons had married, and they seemed to have settled into a new life as a family. For a while everything went well, but then Naomi's husband died. And her two sons died as well. Now Naomi was alone except for her two daughters-in-law, Ruth and Orpah. How could three women survive alone?

Naomi called her daughters-in-law and told them her decision. "I have decided to return to Bethlehem," Naomi said. "I still have relatives there. I am too old to be by myself."

Ruth and Orpah listened sadly. "Each of you should go back to your own families too," Naomi said to them.

Orpah and Ruth did not want to leave Naomi. But Naomi insisted. Finally Orpah decided to do as Naomi asked. She kissed her mother-in-law and then returned to her mother's house.

But Ruth refused to go. "I want to go with you," she told Naomi. "Don't ask me to leave you. You are my family. Where you go, I will go! Your people shall be my people, and your God my God. I will not change my mind!"

Naomi realized that Ruth was serious. Naomi stopped trying to make her stay in Moab, and the two women continued their journey to Bethlehem.

When she arrived in Bethlehem at the beginning of the barley harvest, everyone was surprised to see Naomi again. And everyone was even more surprised to see Naomi's daughter-in-law, Ruth.

Day 1 The more often a child hears a Bible story, the more likely he or she is to remember it. Talk about the story of Ruth and Naomi. Encourage your family to draw a picture of the characters. Remember together that when Ruth went with Naomi, it was one way of saying she had learned to love God as Naomi loved God. Special friends and family can help us grow as faithful followers of God. Read some other stories about special friends and family members in the Bible: Exodus 6:28-30; 7:1-2, 6-7; 1 Samuel 18:1-4; 19:1-7; John 11:1-11; Philippians 1:1; 2:19-22.

Day 2 Draw names for secret pals in your family. Encourage acts of kindness during the week (make up someone's bed, bring in the paper, and so forth). At the end of the week let each person guess who his or her secret pal is.

Day 3 Look through your family albums together. Talk about where various family members now live and how you stay in touch with one another. Is it time for a phone call or a letter?

Day 4 Visit, call, or send a card to an older person in your neighborhood this week, If you visit, encourage your children to talk with the older person about his or her life and interests. Give them a chance to become friends.

Day 5 Tear illustrations out of magazines that show people interacting together. Turn the pictures face down and let each person choose one and make up a friendship story about the picture.

Day 6 Naomi and Ruth had a special friendship. They were also a family. They did things together and showed love and concern for one another. They even worshiped together. Describe your own special friendships. Make three columns on a sheet of paper. Head one: "Our Friends." Head the second one: "How We Met." Head the third one: "How We Show We Are Friends." Add this sheet to your "Wondrous Things" scrapbook.

Day 7 Write the word *friend* across the top of a long sheet of paper. Then work as a family to come up with a word about friends or friendship for each letter of the alphabet. List them vertically on the paper. Let family members decorate the paper and then display it on a wall. You may even want to frame it and give it to a friend. (If this is too difficult, use only the letters of the words *friend* or *friendship*.

A New Family

Talk Point:

Ruth was welcomed, and her baby Obed was loved and cared for by Naomi. God's people praise and thank God for babies and for family.

It was the busy time of harvest. The grain was ripe and ready to be gathered. The workers were in the fields all day cutting down the stalks of barley. Today a newcomer was gleaning in the fields.

Gleaning was the custom in Israel. It was the law that the workers leave any stalks of grain that dropped on the ground. They also left grain around the edges of the field. Then the poor could come and gather grain to provide food for their families.

This newcomer's name was Ruth. She was not from Israel. She came from Moab with her mother-in-law, Naomi. She had not had an easy life. Her husband died in Moab. Now she had come to live in a new country. It was probably hard for her to adjust to all of the new customs she had to learn in Israel.

Ruth worked very hard gathering food for herself and Naomi. Then Boaz came to the field. When he saw Ruth, he was curious. "She is a widow from Moab," his workers told him. "Her mother-in-law is a relative of yours—Naomi. She asked permission to glean so that she could provide food for Naomi."

Boaz called Ruth over, I heard him when he spoke to her. He said, "Ruth, you are welcome to glean in my fields. No one will harm you here. When you are thirsty, drink from the jars of water that my workers provide."

Ruth was amazed at Boaz' generosity. "Why are you being so kind to me, sir?" she asked.

"Because," Boaz replied, "I have heard how kind you have been to Naomi. May the Lord reward you for your deeds."

At mealtime Boaz shared his bread with Ruth. And when she left to return to the fields, Boaz told his workers to leave extra grain behind for her to find.

This story is one with a really happy ending. Boaz and Ruth fell in love and married. They created a happy home for themselves and for Naomi. And it wasn't long before there was a new baby son. They named him Obed. What a happy day!

When Naomi's friends came to visit, they told Naomi that she was very blessed to have such a wonderful family. Naomi took the baby and held him close. She was indeed blessed. She knew that children are a gift from God. Obed was a special baby. He was well cared for by his grandmother and by his parents, Ruth and Boaz.

Day 1 Check the newspaper for stories of people who have done something kind for someone else. Collect the clippings and glue them on a piece of posterboard. Write "Kindness Is Important!" above the pictures. Hang the poster where it can remind family members to be kind to one another.

Day 2 Sponsor a family Kindness Counts Day." Give family members the same number of chocolate kisses or paper hearts. Encourage them to give away a kiss whenever someone does something kind for them. At the end of the day see who has the most kisses. Talk about how it feels to be kind as well as how it feels to be treated kindly.

Day 3 Look for opportunities for your family to share what you can with others. Perhaps you can spend time with someone who is lonely. Maybe you can collect clothes that you have outgrown to give to someone else who needs them. Choose a family project and work together.

Day 4 Visit someone who has just had a baby. Take a gift that your family has made for that family, perhaps a picture frame or a family album.

Day 5 Invite relatives to a family gathering or celebration this week. If you do not have immediate family living near you, invite honorary grandparents from people in the church who help care for your children.

Day 6 Look at family pictures together. Be sure to include pictures of family members as babies. Talk about your happiness when your child was born. Tell your child about the people who helped to take care of him or her. If grandparents are close by, ask them to talk about what it was like waiting for their own children to be born or adopted.

Day 7 Is there a child in your neighborhood or among your friends who is having a difficult time in his or her own family? Perhaps there is a divorce or illness. Make intentional plans to include the child in your family's plans this week.

Vashti's Choice

Scripture:
Esther 1:1-22
Ephesians 5:21, 33

Talk Point:

Although King Ahasuerus treated Queen Vashti with disrespect, she knew that both men and women are people of worth. God expects us to treat all people with respect and love.

Ahasuerus (uh-hash-yoo-ER-uhs) was a powerful king who lived in a huge palace in Susa. He ruled over all of Persia. His kingdom stretched from India to Ethiopia.

One winter Ahasuerus decided to give a banquet to display his great wealth before all the official and leaders of the kingdom. What a party! His guests stayed one hundred and eighty days!

Then he gave another banquet for all the men in the kingdom, not just the officials and leaders. While the king was entertaining his guests, his wife, Queen Vashti (VASH-tigh), gave an equally lavish banquet for all the women.

On the seventh day of the feast, when King Ahasuerus had had more than enough to drink, he commanded that his wife, Queen Vashti, make an appearance before his guests. "Put on your crown. Let them see your beauty," he commanded.

"No!" said Queen Vashti. She was insulted. She did not want to be used as a piece of property for her husband to show off as he might a new chariot. She refused to appear before her husband's guests.

King Ahasuerus was angry. He could not believe that his wife would challenge his authority. After all, in those days women were little more than property. They could not earn their own living. They depended on their fathers or husbands to take care for them. Decisions were made for them by many years of tradition that put men in charge of their lives.

King Ahasuerus consulted his advisors. "What should I do?" he wanted to know. "What should be done to my wife because she has not performed at my command?"

"Her disobedience should be punished," they told him. "Since she refused to appear when her husband called, she must never be allowed into his presence again. After all," they feared, "if Queen Vashti is allowed to disobey her husband, other women may decide that it is okay to rebel!"

So King Ahasuerus passed a law. he decreed that "all women will give honor to their husbands," and every man should be master in his own house."

Vashti's crown was taken from her. She was sent away forever, and the king looked for a new queen.

Day 1

Read Ephesians 5:21 and 33 to find a new rule that governs relationships for people who follow the teachings of Jesus. How can love and respect strengthen a marriage?

Day 2

Hold a family council. Have each family member say something positive about each member of the family. Then make a family covenant. List four or five simple things that people in the family can do to show love and respect for one another. Post the list on the refrigerator. After a week check the list together to find out how your family is doing.

Day 3

Look up the word *respect* in a dictionary. Cut out pictures and words from magazines to make a collage that expresses what the word means.

Day 4

If you wrote a family cheer some weeks ago, shout it now. Can it be adapted to use each family member's name? If not, can you write a simple cheer that can use each family member's name? Briefly review the stories you have read so far. How did the characters in each story treat each other? For instance, did Joseph and his brothers show respect for one another?

Day 5

Look through the pages of a magazine together. What pictures of men and women at work can you find? Make a list of jobs that men and women can do. Explain that in Bible times most women did not work away from home. Ask: "Who have we read about recently who did work outside their homes?" (*Deborah and Ruth*)

Day 6

Donate items to a shelter for battered women in your community. Find out about the services this facility provides and how your family can be supportive.

Day 7

Give each family member a piece of paper, markers, crayons, glue, and glitter. Let each person choose a word that best describes himself or herself and write it on the paper. Decorate the page and add the pages to your "Wondrous Things" scrapbook. Here are some suggestions for words: neat, trustworthy, loyal, caring, kind, honest, loving, friendly, creative, courageous, and intelligent.

A Courageous Woman

Scripture:
Esther 2:2—3:58;
6:1—8:17; 9:26-28
Psalm 46:1

Talk Point:
Esther acted with courage to save her people. With God's help and with the help of others, we can act with courage.

After a while King Ahasuerus grew lonely. His servants suggested that he choose a queen from among the young women in the kingdom.

There was living in Susa at that time a Jewish man named Mordecai. He had raised his cousin, Esther, after her parents died. Now she was a lovely young woman. Mordecai wanted the best for her. When he heard of the king's search for an new queen, he spoke to Esther.

"Esther," he said, "go to the palace to meet the king. Perhaps he will be impressed and will want to marry you. But whatever you do, do not tell anyone that you are Jewish. There are some people who do not like us because of our beliefs."

Just as he hoped, Esther was chosen as the new queen.

One day Mordecai overheard two of the king's servants making plans to kill the king. He hurried to tell Esther, who ran quickly to the king. An investigation was begun. Soon there was proof that Mordecai was right. The king's life had been saved! Esther was delighted.

Not everyone was happy with Mordecai. A man named Haman plotted to get rid of him and all the other Jews who were living in the kingdom. He convinced the king to make a decree that all Jews should be destroyed because they worshiped only God rather than the king.

When Mordecai heard of the plan to kill the Jews, he went to Esther. "Please do not let this happen. Beg the king to spare our lives!"

Esther did not know what to do. "If I go to the king without being called, I may be killed. But if I do not go, I will be killed along with all of my family who are Jews."

"Perhaps it is for just such a time as this that you have become queen," Mordecai said. So Esther went to the king. "Please come to a banquet that I am preparing for you and your advisor Haman."

That night after the banquet King Ahasuerus was reminded of the time when Mordecai had saved his life. He realized that he had never thanked Mordecai. On the next day Haman was dismayed to be chosen to honor Mordecai in the name of the king.

That night King Ahasuerus and Haman went again to a banquet prepared by Queen Esther. This time Esther spoke with courage. "Please, my king, spare the lives of my people, the Jews."

The king realized what Haman had tried to do. He told Mordecai to send letters to allow the Jews to defend themselves so they would not be destroyed. The Jewish people celebrated with joy.

Day 1 Talk with your child about how God works through people. Tell stories you know of people who were in the right place to do the right thing.

Day 2 Select books from your public library that tell about men and women who acted with courage. As you read the stories together, discuss similarities to the story of Esther.

Day 3 Pray together for people who face difficult decisions. Perhaps you or your child will want to name some specific persons who can benefit from your prayers.

Day 4 Plan a family picnic. Visit a monument or marker in your area that celebrates the lives of courageous people.

Day 5 Help your family look through the newspaper to find stories about people who are making a difference in the world by doing what is right. Make a list of the people and what they did. Do you notice extraordinary or ordinary activities?

Day 6 Write a letter to someone in your church or community that your family admires because that person acts with the courage of his or her convictions. Let that person know that he or she is a role model for you and your children.

Day 7 Select an evening and host a "treat your family like royalty" dinner. Have family members fix a special meal, create a centerpiece for the table, and set the table. Choose background music. During the meal talk about what you appreciate about one another.

Faithful Friends

Scripture:
Daniel 1:1-20
Job 34:4a

Talk Point:
In Babylon Daniel and his friends were faithful to the religious laws of Israel. Today we can make choices that are helpful to God's law and to God's will for us.

When King Jehoiakim of Judah ruled, King Nebuchadnezzar from Babylon conquered Jerusalem. The king commanded his palace master to bring some of the Israelites who were smart young men to be servants in Nebuchadnezzar's palace in Babylon.

The king wanted these young men to be well cared for. He even offered them royal portions of rich food and wine. Some of the Hebrew youth—Daniel, Hananiah, Mishael, and Azariah—were given new names. Daniel was called Belteshazzar. Hanamiah was known as Shadrach, Mishael was given the name Meshach, and Azariah was now Abednego.

Daniel knew that the rich foods the king wanted the young men to eat included things that his Jewish religion told him he should not eat. But the palace master, who was responsible for the health and well-being of Daniel and his friends, was afraid he would lose his head if he allowed the young men to eat anything else. But Daniel convinced the man to test them for ten days. Daniel was sure that they would be healthy at the end of the ten days. The four friends ate vegetables and water for ten days. At the end of the time Daniel and his friends were fit and healthy. After this they were given the food they requested and were able to be faithful to God's laws.

To these four, faithful young men God gave knowledge and skill.

Day 1 Plan a healthy, balanced dinner with your family. Let family member choose the entree, the vegetables, and the dessert from choices you provide. Remind your children that choosing and eating the right things makes a healthy body.

Day 2 Challenge your children to think of a specific chore or behavioral goal to work on this week. Provide an incentive for successfully finishing the project.

Day 3 Read the newspaper or watch the TV news together. Look for situations in which people are standing up for their beliefs.

Day 4 Make a list of behaviors or attitudes that are faithful to God. Beside each item name a person whom you associate with the action or beliefs. Talk with your child about ways each of you behaves in ways that are faithful to God. Pray, asking God to help you always respond in a faithful way.

Day 5 Arrange a time for you and your family to interview a dedicated, faithful person from your congregation. Encourage your children to ask about what faith means to this person. (Give the person an idea beforehand of questions your family may ask.) Talk about how this person lives out his or her faith. Ask about any times when the person has been afraid to share beliefs with others. Ask the person to remember your family in prayer.

Day 6 Make a bookmark to keep in your Bible. Every time you read or hear a Bible passage that tells you about being faithful, write the reference or some key words from the verse on your bookmark. Begin by adding this verse: "Let us choose what is right" (Job 34:4a).

Day 7 Encourage family members to write a postcard to Daniel, telling him about an issue of faithfulness they have had to deal with, and how they responded with faithfulness to God. Add the postcards to your "Wondrous Things" scrapbook.

In the Lions' Den

Scripture:
Daniel 6:1-23, 25-28
Psalm 121:2

Talk Point:
Daniel prayed to God daily, even though praying placed his life in danger. Daniel trusted God, and we can trust God today too.

Listen to the story of a man well known
Because his faith and trust in God was bravely shown.

When Daniel very highly with the king did rate,
Others were so jealous that they planned his fate.

They came up with a law that said for thirty days
Only to the king could people pray and praise.

If anyone should pray to one besides the king,
That person in the lions' den the king would fling.

When Daniel heard about the plot, to God he prayed.
Someone ran to tell the king—"Daniel's disobeyed!"

Then Daniel right away was put into the pit.
King Darius did not approve, no, not a bit.

The law was set, so there was nothing he could do.
He said to Daniel, "May your God deliver you!"

The next day when the king came by at morning light,
What he saw before his eyes was quite a sight.

There was Daniel sitting with the lions' mouths shut;
Not a single bruise or bite, a scratch or cut.

Marveling at Daniel, who in God did trust,
The king proclaimed from here on out his kingdom must

Bow down before the one true God; "He'll be our guide;
Daniel's God we'll worship now," he loudly cried.

And so that ends the story of a man well known
Because his faith and trust in God was bravely shown.

Day 1 Visit a zoo, if there is one in your area. Remember Daniel in the lion's den when you visit the lions. If a trip to the zoo is not possible, rent a video about lions.

Day 2 Daniel prayed three times a day. Encourage your family to pray together before each meal this week.

Day 3 Make a list of things in your home that you trust will work when you need them (such as the light switch). Talk about how important it is to learn to trust God.

Day 4 Go to the library to find books about people who have overcome difficulties. Tell your child stories about people in your family or in your community who have faced their fears with God's help. Remind your child that God is always near.

Day 5 Have each family member write down something that he or she has learned from another person that he or she values. Perhaps it is something about himself or herself, advice about how to treat others, or a saying that has helped him or her understand life.

Day 6 Make a growth chart for each child's life so far. Draw a vertical line and mark off inches. Put the height and age beside the proper designation. Add to the chart when your child learned and began doing certain things, such as walking, talking, reading, and so forth. Talk with your child about the people who have helped him or her learn. Include parents, grandparents, friends, teachers, and so forth. Say a prayer thanking God for all these people.

Day 7 Make a special effort to befriend someone who is new in your neighborhood or in your church. Make cookies or a pie to take to the new friend.

Jonah

Talk Point:
God called Jonah to go to Nineveh, but Jonah ran away. Yet, when Jonah prayed, God helped him.

God forgave the people of Nineveh when they changed their ways. God loves us so much that, even when we do wrong, God forgives and helps us.

My name is Jonah. One day God asked me to go to the city of Nineveh and tell the people who lived there to change their ways.

I thought about it for awhile. I decided that Nineveh must be truly evil if God wanted the people there to change. I decided I would not go.

I knew God would not like my decision, so I ran in the opposite direction to hide from God! I went to Joppa and got on a boat to go to Tarshish. I thought, *God can just find someone else to go to Nineveh!*

After we left the port, I went below deck and fell asleep. I thought that I had escaped. But God found me. God sent such a strong wind that the storm threatened to destroy the very boat that I was on.

The boat's crew began to throw things overboard to keep the ship afloat. Then finally the captain came below deck and asked me how I could sleep when all our lives were in danger. He told me to pray to God so that the boat would be spared from destruction.

I knew the storm was my fault. It isn't possible to run away from God. "Throw me overboard," I told them, "and the storm will stop."

The sailors didn't want to throw me overboard, but finally they had no choice. When they threw me into the sea, the storm stopped.

I knew I was in trouble because I had disobeyed God. But then a strange thing happened. I can hardly believe it even now. A big fish came and swallowed me! I sat inside that fish for three days and three nights. Let me tell you—I had plenty of time to think!

Finally I cried out to God, and God heard me. I promised to do whatever God asked of me. Then the fish coughed me up onto dry land! God told me a second time to go to Nineveh, and I obeyed.

When I got there, I told the people to repent. I didn't expect them to listen to me. But I was amazed! Even the king was convinced that the city would be destroyed if they did not obey.

So the people of Nineveh changed, but I didn't. I still wanted God to destroy them. After all, they deserved it! I was so mad! I went outside the city and sat under a shelter I built. God provided a bush to give me shade, but then a worm attached the bush and it died! Then a strong, dry wind and the hot sun made me sick. O God, why?

God reminded me that as I cared about the bush, God cared about the people and animals living in Nineveh. God did not want them to be destroyed, so God forgave them.

Day 1 Look through the Bible together or recall stories you have already read about people who heard God's call. Find stories about people such as Noah, Moses, Samuel, Jeremiah, John the Baptist, and Paul.

Day 2 Start an encouragement jar. Place a marble in the jar each time someone in the family does something loving or caring for another person. Make plans for a special family celebration when the jar is filled.

Day 3 Tell your child about a time when you needed to know that you could trust God to be with you to help. Encourage your child to talk to you about a time when he or she has asked God for help. Talk about why it is important to trust that God hears our prayers, especially in hard times.

Day 4 Make a list of people who are difficult to love. Accept any names your child adds to the list. Pray together for these people by name during the week. Take some time to talk about the good things you and your child know about each person. Remind your child that God's love is for everyone—especially for the special people you are praying for!

Day 5 Make a prayer chain out of construction paper strips. Write on each link the name of a person or a group of people your family will pray for. Each day remove one link from the chain as your family prays for that person or group.

Day 6 As a family learn more about a community project that helps others. Then decide how your family can participate in some way in the project. Talk with one another about why it is important for Christians to show God's love to others.

Day 7 Plant a flower or herb. Encourage your child to take care of the plant. Remind your child that God cares for each person in your family, in your church, and all over the world.

Samuel Remembers

Oh, I remember my mother, Hannah. She was the first one who taught me about serving God. In fact, she promised God that if I could be born, I would belong to God as long as I lived. My mother was a faithful woman.

When I was growing up helping Eli in the temple, I learned that God was calling me to do an important job. So I chose to be what my mother and God wanted me to be—like you do today when you choose to live as Jesus taught. Your parents may help you, but you must choose.

God called me to be a judge; and I chose to be trustworthy, fair, and just. You see, in Bible times the Hebrew people did not have presidents, or prime ministers, or even governors to help them. But when the people realized that they needed leaders to help them know how to live, God chose judges—like me.

Now we judges were not like the judges you know today. We traveled around. We listened to people's problems, and we helped them know what God wanted them to do. As a judge I always tried to make fair decisions.

I remember one time when the people listened to what I said. It was when the Philistines wanted to take the Promised Land away from us. Unfortunately some of the Hebrews were building temples and worshiping golden statues there—just like the Philistines did. God had sent me to be the leader, so I warned them. "Throw the statues away," I said. "There is only one God. If we are not faithful, the Philistines will destroy us."

God was with me, and the people respected me as a leader chosen by God. So they listened. We built an altar to God. While we were asking for forgiveness, the Philistines attacked. I prayed for forgiveness for the people and asked for God's protection. God answered my prayer. God forgave the people, and they were able to drive the Philistines away.

Day 1 Encourage family members to find a way to do a loving thing for someone else. Perhaps you can visit a sick friend or prepare loving notes to leave where other family members will find them.

Day 2 Suggest that younger family members draw a picture of their teacher (either ar school or in Sunday school). The picture can be a thank-you gift to the one who leads your child. Older children and adults could write a thank-you note to a teacher.

Day 3 Talk with your family about prayer. Help children know that prayer is one important way that Christians can discover what God wants them to do. Pray daily as a family.

Day 4 Ask your child if he or she knows someone at school who is treated unfairly or left out of the group. Help your child think about what God would want him or her to do. Will it make a difference in the way the left-out child is treated?

Day 5 Tell your family stories about your own childhood. Was there a special teacher or other person you respected as a leader? Tell your family what made that person special.

Day 6 Talk to your child about your job. Talk about how what you do is a way of answering God's call and serving God. Ask your child: "What would you like to be when you grow up?" Let him or her tell you why. Encourage your child to think of many possibilities. Talk about how each possibility might be a way to serve God.

Day 7 Help your child find a way to serve in the family during the week. Perhaps he or she can help clean up after a meal, help clean out the basement, or read a story to a younger brother or sister. Talk about how serving others is an important way to serve God. Thank your child and lift up his or her name in a thankful prayer.

Give Us a King!

Scripture:
1 Samuel 8:1-22;
10:17-26; 12:13-15

Talk Point:
God chose Saul to be the first king of Israel. In Bible times and today, leaders and the people they lead are all called to obey and to serve God.

It was not always easy being a judge. Sometimes the people asked me to do things that I did not agree with. And sometimes it wasn't easy to know what God wanted me to do.

There was one time when I really didn't know what to do for a while. I was getting old when the people said to me, "Samuel, everyone else has a king. We want a king too."

I knew that just because everyone else was doing something, that was not a good reason for us to do it. But even when I reminded them, "God is your king," they were not satisfied.

So I prayed. God didn't think the people needed a king either. But God didn't say no. God told me to warn the people about what would happen if they chose a human king. The people still insisted, though. "Give us a king!" they said. So God sent me to Mizpah, where we cast lots.

"The tribe of Benjamin," I said when the first of the lots was cast. Then the lot fell to the family of Matrites (MAY-trights) in the tribe of Benjamin. Finally I called out, "Saul, for the family of Matrites. Saul will be king."

At first we couldn't find Saul. He was hiding. I guess he knew what a great responsibility it was to be a leader. He wasn't at all sure he wanted to be the king. But God showed us where he was. And when he came forward, the people shouted, "Long live the king!"

"It's important for the king to be a strong leader," I told them. I even wrote down the rights and duties of a king so they would remember.

I still don't think that giving the people a king was a good thing. But God granted the people's request. And all their lives were changed. Some kings were good and did what God wanted them to do. But others forgot about God. The one thing they could be sure of, though, was that God would always be with them—even if they made mistakes.

Day 1 Read again 1 Samuel 9:27—10:1 and talk about its implications for us as Christians. This passage tells us that Samuel anointed Saul with oil (poured oil on his head) to show that Saul was the new king. Anointing became a traditional symbol of kingship for the people of Israel. When they looked for the one God would send to deliver them, they looked for an anointed one, a messiah. When Jesus came, he became known as the Christ because Christ is the Greek translation of the Hebrew word *Messiah*.

Day 2 Continue to talk about leaders and leadership, but lighten the mood by playing a rousing game of "Follow the Leader!"

Day 3 Be sure your child sees you using your Bible every day. Even if you read the Bible story from this devotional book or another Bible storybook, open your Bible to the correct passage and show it to your children. If your older child likes to read aloud, encourage him or her to read at least part of the passage from the Bible.

Day 4 If you have older children, have fun using a concordance. If you do not have a complete concordance, most Bibles have a brief one in the back. Look up the word *king* and compare Old Testament and New Testament verses. Think of other words. You may want to write up one or two examples for your "Wondrous Things" scrapbook.

Day 5 Make paper crowns and wear them at meals during the week. Talk about the important qualities of being a good leader. Encourage one another to be strong, honest, kind, and faithful.

Day 6 Plan for a pretend overnight trip. What would you take? What would you pack to eat on the way? What choices have to be made? If possible, let everyone sleep in the family room. What difficulties do you have to overcome going to sleep and getting up in the morning?

Day 7 Write a prayer for the leaders in your church, community, city, and nation. Encourage each family member to contribute one name to the list.

David, the Shepherd

Scripture:
1 Samuel 6:13
Psalm 23

Talk Point:
David cared for his father's sheep. God promises to be with us to help us do our work well.

What a day! I can hardly believe what's happened in just one day. One minute I was out it in the fields watching the sheep. Then the next minute someone was telling me that I am going to be the next king of Israel! What a day!

Let me tell you about it. I'm David. Every day I take care of my father's sheep. I love being a shepherd. It feels good knowing that the sheep depend on me. They trust me to take care of them—even when they do dumb things like falling off a cliff. And it feels good to know that my father trusts me to do a good job.

It's not all hard work, though. Sometimes when things are quiet, I like to play my lyre and sing. Sometimes I even write songs. In fact, I wrote one about how God takes care of me the same way I take care of my father's sheep. I like to think of God as my shepherd. I know that God will take care of me—even when I do dumb things.

But today the strangest thing happened. My father sent for me. It's not good to leave the sheep for long, so I knew it must be important. I went quickly.

Samuel was there. I'd heard of him before. I knew he was a man of God. But I never guessed why he wanted to see me! He said that God had sent him to my father's house to find the person who would be the next king after Saul died.

I could hardly believe it when he said God had chosen me. My brothers are all older and stronger than I am. I'm just a young shepherd boy. But someone told me that Samuel had already seen each of my brothers, and then he had sent for me.

I'm not the king yet. Saul will be king as long as he lives. But Samuel says that God wants me to be the king later. What a day!

Day 1 Read these verses from David's psalms to discover what God saw in David's heart. Psalm 4:3; 7:10, 17; 18:1; 33:1-3; 37:3a; 51:10; 63:1-4; and 92:1-5. Family members may wish to choose one of these passages to illustrate. Put the illustrations in your "Wondrous Things" scrapbook.

Day 2 Let a younger child take a turn at doing a task or chore that has always fallen to an older person. Praise the effort lavishly.

Day 3 As David cared for the sheep, he grew to love God's creation. Take a walk together. Or sit in your yard or in a park. Talk with your family about the wonders of God's creation. Give thanks to God.

Day 4 Let your children tell you what it means to "look on the heart" as God does. Talk about what God will see in your heart and what is in your child's heart. Cut out hearts and print 1 Samuel 16:7c on them. Send them to people you love. Tell your child a wonderful thing you see in his or her heart.

Day 5 Tradition suggests that David's shield may have been in the shape of a six-pointed star. Since David was one of the best known of the kings of Israel, the Star of David is often used as a symbol of the Jewish people. Today the Star of David is on the flag of Israel, the Jewish nation. The Star of David is different from the star that we usually use at Christmas to point the way to Jesus' birth in Bethlehem. However, the six-pointed star made from two three-sided triangles is used by Christians as a symbol of the Trinity. Glue together three flat craft sticks to make a triangle. Make at least six triangles. Glue one triangle upside down over another and glue the two together to make a star. Loop a piece of yarn through the top of one star and tie the ends to make a loop for hanging. Add several other stars by tying them together with yarn. Hang your mobile where you can see it and be reminded of David.

Day 6 Read Psalm 23 together. List the ways God cared for the shepherd. List the ways God cares for us. Add to your "Wondrous Things" scrapbook.

Day 7 Celebrate! Wear your crowns to dinner to honor David, the shepherd who became a king. For dessert decorate a cake to look like a crown.

Praise and Friendship

Talk Point:

David wrote psalms of praise for God's presence and care. God has given us many abilities to enjoy and to use in helping others. David and Jonathan were friends who loved and cared for each other. God wants us to be good friends and to have good friends.

Crash! Bang! What a noise King Saul made! He was so angry that his face turned dark red. He screamed at all of his servants, and he threw a water jar across the room. He had been this way ever since Samuel told him that God was going to choose someone else to be king. One minute he would be laughing and happy, and the next minute he would be angry and unhappy.

One of his servants had heard of a young shepherd named David who played his lyre to calm his sheep. The people of King Saul's household decided to send for David to see if his music could calm King Saul.

That is how David came to live in King Saul's court. He had not been there very long when King Saul had another bad time. As soon as he started shouting and throwing things, David reached for his lyre and began to play and sing. It worked! Almost at once King Soul calmed down and felt better.

David stayed on in King Saul's court. Soon the king learned that David was a good leader and put him in charge of part of his army. At first Saul was happy, but then people started calling David a hero and paying more attention to him than to Saul. King Saul was jealous. He made plans to get rid of David.

David had become a very good friend of Jonathan, King Saul's son. Jonathan was sorry that King Saul had begun to dislike David. When he overheard the king planning to get rid of David, he ran to his friend.

"David, David," he said, "my father is planning to hurt you. I've come to warn you."

"What should I do?" David asked.

"Hide in the field," Jonathan replied. "I will come with a message. No matter what happens, please remain a faithful friend to me and all my family forever."

"I promise," David said. "I will always love and care for your family."

The next day Jonathan went to the field to warn his friend. They both cried and hugged each other. "Go in peace," Jonathan said to David. "May the Lord be with us and our descendants forever!"

Day 1 Talk with your child about things he or she does especially well (sing, study, share, talk politely, play a sport, and so forth). Help him or her recognize these as special abilities. Discover the special abilities in each member of your family.

Day 2 Sing together a song that is special to your child. Then teach your child a song that is special to you.

Day 3 As your family starts the day or gets ready for bed at night, play cheerful, gentle music to set a happy tone. This could become a bedtime ritual for your children to help them settle down and go to sleep peacefully.

Day 4 Music influences our attitudes and thoughts. Take time to listen to the music your elementary and middle school students prefer. Listen to the lyrics together. Ask your child what the lyrics mean. If they are inappropriate, help your child select some music by a well-known Christian artist to enjoy.

Day 5 Talk about what it means to be friends. Help your child remember that adults—including parents and teachers—can be their friends too. Help your child think about friends who may not go to church. Is there someone he or she can invite to Sunday school next week?

Day 6 Tell your child about some special friends in your life. Help your child understand that having friends and being a friend are important things. Talk about your child's best friend. What does he or she like about the friend? What do they do together? How do they let each other know that they like being friends? Pray with your child, asking God for strong friendships now and in the future.

Day 7 Let your child invite one or more friends to spend the night. Fix them a special treat. Invite them to make acrostics using their first names and the word *friends*.

God's People United

Scripture:
2 Samuel 2:1-11;
5:1-5; 6:1-5, 12-15,
17-19
Psalm 133:1

Talk Point:
With God's help King David made Israel a strong and united nation. God will be with children and adults today as they do the work God calls them to do.

"**G**o to Hebron in Judah," David heard God say. David had just received the message that King Saul and his son Jonathan had both been killed in battle.

"Oh, my friend Jonathan," grieved David. "I will remember my promise of faithful love to your family. Now it is time for me to become king."

The people of Judah welcomed David as their king, but in the Northern Kingdom people were still loyal to Saul's son Ishbosheth, who had become king there in his father's place. For seven and a half years there was conflict. But Ishbosheth was finally defeated, and the people of the Northern Kingdom turned to David.

"Even when Saul was our king, you were the one who led us," they said. "We know that God has chosen you to be a shepherd over all the people of Israel. We want you to be our king too."

So David became the king of one kingdom—just as it had been when Saul was king.

"Hebron is too far south," David decided. "I am going to make Jerusalem the capital city of our United Kingdom." And soon the city of Jerusalem became known as "the city of David."

God is with us, thought David. *We must bring the Ark of the Covenant to our capital city and give it a place of honor.*

"Make a joyful noise unto the Lord!" the people shouted when they saw the Ark coming into Jerusalem. David sang and danced with joy.

Mephibosheth (mi-FIB-oh-sheth), the son of Jonathan was afraid, however. King David had sent for him. *I am probably going to die,* he thought.

Mephibosheth moved slowly as he approached King David's throne. He was only five years old when his father and grandfather had been killed in battle. A nurse saved his life, but in her rush to hide him, Mephibosheth had fallen. Both of his feet had been injured. Now he could not walk without the help of crutches.

"Don't be afraid," David told the young man. "You won't be harmed."

Then David told Mephibosheth of the friendship he had shared with Jonathan. "I promised your father that I would always be faithful to our friendship by caring for his family. I want to keep that promise. All of the land that belonged to your grandfather, Saul, is now yours. And you will always be welcome at the table in my home."

Day 1 As your family prays this week, remember the needs for peace around the world. Find Israel on a map or a globe. Pray especially for peace in Israel.

Day 2 Talk about unity within your family. Are there ways you can practice unity? Help your children see that getting along with brothers and sisters, helping one another without fussing, and being polite are examples of unity. Use Psalm 133:1 as a special family verse each day this week.

Day 3 Encourage your older child to practice using a concordance. Help him or her find and read Bible verses that talk about peace.

Day 4 If possible, visit a shelter with your family. Offer to help. Perhaps you and your family can help serve a meal.

Day 5 Consider things your family can celebrate together—the beauty of a sunny day, a new friend at school, a job well done, and so forth. Add this list to your "Wondrous Things" scrapbook.

Day 6 Visit your local library. Look for stories about persons with disabilities. When we do not understand, many of us may have uncomfortable feelings around persons who have disabilities. Talk with your child about ways to be kind and loving. Be prepared to answer your child's questions. Pray with your child for the special needs of a friend or someone at school

Day 7 Make kindness placemats. Draw the outline of your hand on each side of a sheet of construction paper. On one side write the first part of the Bible verse, "Those who are kind reward themselves" (Proverbs 11:17). On the other side write a promise about how you will be kind to someone else—a brother or sister, a friend, a parent or child, or someone at school. Cover both sides of your placemat with clear, self-adhesive paper. Tell your family: When you use your placemat, place the Bible verse side facing up. Only you will know what promise is written on the other side. Each time you use your placemat, remember your promise to be kind.

Wise King Solomon

Scripture:
1 Kings 2:1-4, 10-12;
3:1-14; 5:1-12;
6:7, 11-31, 38;
8:1-26, 54-61
Psalm 122:1

Talk Point:
King Solomon built a Temple and dedicated it to God. We are glad to have churches, special places to learn about God and to worship God.

"**Y**ou must be strong. You must have courage. And most of all, you must obey God." With these words David advised his son Solomon of the things he would need when he became king. And that would not be long, for King David was old.

"If you and your children remain faithful to the Lord," David said, "the Lord will bless our family, and the throne of Israel will be strong."

When Solomon became the new king, God asked him, "What gift would you ask from me?"

Solomon answered, "Give me wisdom; give me an understanding mind so that I may rule wisely. Help me to know the difference between good and evil." And God gave Solomon more wisdom than any king had ever had or ever would have!

Wise King Solomon remembered his father's wish for a house for the Lord in Jerusalem. "I will build the Temple my father dreamed of," Solomon decided. "It will be a home for the Ark of the Covenant to remind us that God is always with us."

"Be faithful, and obey all that I have commanded," God said to Solomon. "If you will keep my commandments, I will establish with you the promise I made to your father David—I will always dwell among the children of Israel."

After seven years the Temple was completed. It was magnificent. On the outside two tall bronze pillars stood beside the door. Inside the walls were carved from cedar and covered with gold. And there was a special place—the most holy place—for the Ark of the Covenant. And all the things that had been dedicated by King David were brought into the treasuries of the house of the Lord.

"The Lord has kept the promise made to my father David," said Solomon. "In the Temple there is a place for the Ark of God that contains the covenant God made with our ancestors when he brought them out of the land of Egypt. The Lord's promise has been fulfilled. God will never forsake the people of Israel."

Then Solomon made an offering to God and blessed the people of Israel. "Devote yourselves completely to the Lord our God," he challenged them.

Day 1   Read 1 Kings 2:2b-3a. Then encourage family members to write David's advice to his son Solomon in their own words. Is David's advice valuable for us today? Add your papers to your "Wondrous Things" scrapbook.

Day 2   Sign up to help at a cleanup day at your church. Or let your family volunteer to do some special task together for the church. Remind your children that we are responsible for God's house.

Day 3   Ride or walk by several church buildings with your family. Talk about how each one is different. What materials is each building made from? How big is it? Is it fancy or plain? Talk about what makes all church buildings alike. Remember together that it is people who love and serve God together that make a church.

Day 4   Talk with your child about the churches of your childhood. What did the building look like? What did the people do? If you have older relatives who live close by, plan a visit to talk about the churches of their childhood. If you have older relatives who live far away, write them a letter asking about the churches of their childhood.

Day 5   Encourage your child to tell you what he or she likes best about his or her church. Why? What would he or she like to change? Encourage your children to draw pictures of your church. Use the pictures for note paper to write to friends or relatives.

Day 6   The people of Israel called the Temple "a house for God, a dwelling place for God in their midst." The new Temple was treated with respect. In 1 Corinthians 3:16-17 Paul describes each person as God's temple. Read this passage and then discuss with your family how we treat our bodies. For instance, do you eat well-balanced meals, exercise regularly, and so on?

Day 7   Talk about promises. If you have been using this book straight through, see how many promises or covenants your family can remember. What is the best promise of all?

The Coming Messiah

Scripture:
Isaiah 9:6-7
Jeremiah 33:14-16

Talk Point:
God promised that one of David's descendants would be a special king, a Messiah, who would bring justice and righteousness and peace. We know that special person was Jesus.

The days are surely coming, says the Lord." Everyone listened closely to hear what Jeremiah might say. "In those days and at that time I will cause a righteous Branch to spring up for David; and he shall execute justice and righteousness in the land."

"What's that mean?" Joshua asked his sister Miriam. "Who is David? What kind of Branch is he talking about?"

Miriam answered as much as she knew. "David was a mighty king of Israel many years ago. The priests say that God promised that someday one of David's ancestors would come to save us. He is the one called the Messiah. I think he is supposed to be a strong and mighty king—maybe even more mighty than David."

"A new king? One who will save us from the problems we are having now in Jerusalem? That would be great!" Joshua didn't know much about what was happening in Jerusalem, but he did know that his father was worried that they might have to leave. "Let's ask Father about this new king," Joshua suggested.

When Joshua's father heard his children's question, he looked as if he had a wonderful story to tell. "Sit down," he urged them. "Let me tell you what God has promised" The prophet Isaiah said, 'A shoot shall come out from the stump of Jesse, and a branch shall grow out of his roots.'"

"That's just as strange as what Jeremiah said," moaned Joshua. "But Jeremiah was talking about David, not somebody named Jesse."

"Yes, they are strange-sounding words," said Joshua's father, "but they mean the same thing. Jesse was David's father. The prophets are telling us that someday God will send a messiah, a messiah who is a descendant of King David—and of his father Jesse."

"Wow!" said Miriam. "That's great. That means that even though things seem bad for Jerusalem right now, someday a messiah will come to save us."

"That's right," answered Father. And then he began to tell them some other things that the prophet Isaiah had said.

"For a son has been born for us,/ a son given to us;
authority rests upon his shoulders;/ and he is named
Wonderful Counselor, Mighty God,/ Everlasting Father, Prince of Peace.
His authority will grow continually,/ and there shall be endless peace
for the throne of David and his kingdom."

Because this is the transition between the Old Testament and the New Testament, use this week to make a Jesse Tree to help your family understand the connection between the promises/covenants in the Old Testament and the fulfilling of the promise in Jesus.

You will need the following pictures for your ornaments: an Old Testament prophet (since many of these men were shepherds, you can probably find a picture of a shepherd to use); stone tablets; sheep or lamb; crown and scepter; and a manger. Your family can draw these symbols or find them in old copies of your Sunday school curriculum or on Christmas cards.

Center a bare tree branch in a clay flower pot or other container. You may want to spray paint the branch with gold paint, or leave it in its natural state.

Explain the symbols: The sheep and the crown and scepter stand for David, the shepherd boy who became a king; the tables of the law stand for the Hebrew people, who early in their history entered into a covenant with God to be God's people. when God gave Moses the Ten Commandments; the Old Testament prophet stands for those who spoke God's promise to send a Messiah. The baby Jesus is the fulfillment of that promise.

Encourage your family to make as many of the ornaments as they wish and to hang them on the tree branch. While you work, you may have someone read through all the promises you have studied so far. Another suggestion would be to look in your hymnal to find hymns and readings about the promised coming of the Messiah. These might be listed under "Promised Coming,'" "Advent," or Jesus Christ—Promised Coming." Many of these hymns are unfamiliar to most of us, but if they are read as poetry, they can be very enjoyable for your family. Two particularly good ones that build on the stories you have just finished are "Hail to the Lord's Anointed" and "Blessed Be the God of Israel." If you do not have a hymnal at home, or if these hymns are not in your hymnal, ask your choir director if he or she can help you find them.

Name Him Jesus

Scripture:
Isaiah 7:14
Luke 1:26-38
Matthew 1:18-24

Talk Point:
People in Bible times looked forward to the birth of the Messiah. We celebrate Jesus' birth and remember the promises of God.

It was just like any other day. Mary was busy with her work, probably thinking about the day she would marry Joseph. then suddenly, as quick as you can blink, an angel appeared. Mary didn't know what to think.

The angel Gabriel spoke. "Greetings, favored one. The Lord is with you. Do not be afraid. You are going to have a baby and you will name him Jesus. Your baby, Jesus, will be called the Son of God."

"But I'm not married," answered Mary.

"Don't worry," replied the angel. "The Holy Spirit will come, and the baby will be God's Son."

While Mary was trying to understand what she had heard, the angel continued, "Elizabeth, your relative who is very old, will also have a baby. For you see, nothing is impossible with God."

Then as quickly as he had appeared, Gabriel was gone. Mary was alone with much to think about.

When Joseph heard that Mary was going to have a baby, he was upset. *What should I do? Should I send her away? Should I divorce her? I don't want her to suffer, but surely I cannot marry her now,* he thought. Joseph fell asleep wondering how he would handle this problem.

While Joseph slept, an angel appeared to him in a dream. "Joseph, don't be afraid to marry Mary. The baby she will have is a part of God's plan. The child is from the Holy Spirit. You will name him Jesus, because he will save people from their sins. Do you remember what Isaiah the prophet said? He told about a young woman whose baby would be known by many names. One of those names is Emmanuel, which means "God with us." This baby will be the Son of God. Marry Mary. Everything will work out."

When Joseph awoke, he hurried to find Mary. Soon they were married, and they waited eagerly for the birth of God's Son, Jesus.

Day 1 Talk with your child about how his or her name was chosen. Tell about other special names in your family. If there are unusual names in your family tree, talk about them. If you know why they were chosen, share that information with your family.

Day 2 Isaiah and other prophets told the Hebrew people that one day God would send a messiah, a savior. How many descriptions can you find in the Book of Isaiah to describe the coming Messiah? Read Isaiah 7:14; 9:6-7; 40:11; 41:14; and 42:1. Decorate a page for your "Wondrous Things" scrapbook with the names of the Messiah.

Day 3 Read more Isaiah passages to find out the work the Messiah would do: Isaiah 42:1; 52:7; and 61:1, 2b.

Day 4 Talk to your child about Mary and Joseph. Emphasize that they were obedient to God. Remind them that they can be obedient to God by listening to their parents, their teachers, and their pastor.

Day 5 If you are using these lessons at Christmas time, go shopping together for a family Christmas card. Try to choose one that will tell people how your family feels about the birth of Christ. If you are using these lessons at another time of the year, begin to plan to make your own cards. Let each family member suggest what the cover might look like.

Day 6 Think of a simple message for your family Christmas cards. What would you most like to convey to your friends?

Day 7 Go through your Christmas card list. Are there new friends who need to be added to the list? Pray for each family on your list.

Mary and Elizabeth Praise God

Scripture:
Luke 1:36-49, 56

Talk Point:
Mary told Elizabeth about the coming birth of Jesus and gave thanks to God. We too thank God for Jesus.

I will never forget the day I found out that I was going to have a baby. My husband, Zechariah, and I were getting old. We had almost given up hope of having children. But God blessed us and sent us a son—a special son. Our son would be the one to prepare the way for the Messiah that God had promised to send. Our people, the Hebrew people, had been waiting for so long.

And then before my baby—whom we named John—was born, my relative Mary from Nazareth came to see me. I was surprised to see her, but I soon knew that God had sent her. She had wonderful news.

Even before Mary told me, somehow I knew that she was going to be the mother of the Messiah. My baby knew it too, although I still don't understand how. "Blessed are you among women," I told her.

I know Mary must have been afraid. After all, she and Joseph were not married yet. She must have worried about what people would think. And she was so young! Having a baby would be news enough, but to be the mother of God's Son was a real blessing and an awesome responsibility. But Mary's faith was strong. I could see why God had chosen her to be the mother of the Messiah. Even in her uncertainty about the future, Mary sang praises to God for blessing her.

I can still remember Mary's song. She sang:

> My soul magnifies the Lord
>   and my spirit rejoices in God my Savior,
> for he has looked with favor on the lowliness
>   of his servant.
> Surely from now on all generations will
>   call me blessed,
> for the Mighty One has done great things for me,
>   and holy is his name.

Mary stayed with us for three months, helping me as the time for my baby's birth came nearer. Then she returned home to Joseph so that they could wait together for the time when her special baby would be born. Waiting is probably the hardest part!

Day 1 Traditions are customs that are passed from generation to generation. Cultures have traditions; groups have traditions; families have traditions. Important values, beliefs, and ideas are passed on through traditions. Traditions help people remember and celebrate the things that are important to them. What are the traditions in your family that center around preparing for the birth of Jesus? Ask your family for ideas for new traditions that they would like to start.

Day 2 Give each family member several wooden craft sticks. Lay the craft sticks side-by-side so that the edges of the sticks are touching. People with long names will need more sticks. Put a strip of masking tape across the top and bottom of the sticks. Using a marker with a thick tip, write your name across the sticks, being sure that each letter is divided so that part of it is on at least two sticks. Turn the sticks over and write the name *Jesus* on the other side of the sticks. (Use a different color marker to keep the two sides of the puzzle separate. Or use the same color marker to make the puzzles more challenging.) Remove the masking tape. Mix up the sticks. Then put the puzzles together to spell your name on one side and Jesus' name on the other side.

Day 3 Encourage family members to act out the story of Mary and Elizabeth.

Day 4 Talk about how your child's mother told other the good news when she was expecting a baby or preparing to adopt a baby. Who did she tell?

Day 5 Help your child make a small treat for a church member who is sick.

Day 6 Sing Christmas songs (even if it is July!) as a family. Enjoy the secular Christmas songs your children like, as well as the carols that tell about Jesus' birth.

Day 7 Help your child choose a baby item to take to a shelter.

A Manger Bed

Talk Point:

Jesus, the baby promised by God, was born in Bethlehem. When we celebrate Jesus' birth, we remember that God loves us and all people.

Before Jesus was born, the emperor ordered all the people to register in their family's hometown so that taxes could be collected. So Mary and Joseph set out on a trip to Bethlehem, which was about seventy miles away. Since Mary would have her baby soon, traveling would be slow.

"No! There is absolutely no place for you to stay," said the innkeeper when Mary and Joseph arrived in the crowded city of Bethlehem.

"But Mary is tired. Her baby will be born soon. There must be somewhere for her to rest," Joseph pleaded.

"Well, there is the stable," said the innkeeper. "You are right. She must have somewhere to rest. You are welcome to make a bed in the straw."

Joseph took Mary to a quiet corner of the stable and gathered a pile of straw. Then he gently laid a blanket over the straw to make a bed for Mary. There in the stable they slept.

Before the night was over, Mary had given birth to a beautiful baby boy. She washed the baby and wrapped bands of cloth around his little body to keep him warm. Mary and Joseph were very happy, even though they had to lay their newborn baby in a manger.

Mary and Joseph named the baby Jesus, just as the angel Gabriel had told them to do. They smiled when they remembered that the name *Jesus* means "God saves." They quietly praised God for this wonderful gift—a baby named Jesus.

Day 1

Talk about what that first Christmas must have been like for Mary and Joseph. Help your child imagine what it would be like to be born in a barn. If possible, visit a barn. List the things you hear, see, and smell.

Day 2

Watch a Christmas video together.

Day 3

Use the Internet or library books to research the area where Jesus was born. Find Nazareth and Bethlehem on a map. How does the weather in Bethlehem compare with the weather in your town?

Day 4

Notice homeless families you and your child may see in the community. Talk about what being homeless means and what you can do to help. Find out about organizations in your area that help people who are homeless and hungry. If the churches in your area have a "Room in the Inn" project, help your children make the connection between Jesus' birth and caring for the homeless.

Day 5

Talk to your child about giving gifts. Instead of asking, "What do you want for Christmas?", ask "What will you give for Christmas?"

Day 6

Visit a homeless shelter with your family. Take a gift of blankets or warm socks.

Day 7

If you have clothes your children wore as infants, get them out and admire them. Talk about how differently we dress our children than Mary would have dressed Jesus. Talk about how we bathe and care for our children. Mary would have bathed Jesus and then rubbed salt on his legs and arms before wrapping him in long strips of soft cloth. Bible-times people believed that the salt helped the legs grow straight and strong. What things do we do today to be sure our children have healthy bodies?

A Savior Is Born!

Scripture:
Luke 2:8-20

Talk Point:
Shepherds praise God for the gift of Jesus. A part of celebrating Christmas is praising God for the peace, love, and joy that Jesus brings.

It was a cold night on the hillside near Bethlehem. The sheep on the hillside had been counted and were safely in their folds. The shepherds gathered near the campfire to keep warm. It was a dark night, and the shepherds lay quietly listening to the baas of the lambs, the crackling of the campfire, and the singing of the crickets.

Suddenly—a bright light and beautiful music were everywhere! One by one the shepherds sat up, startled from their dreams by the unexpected brightness of the star that lit up the sky.

"What's that?" one of them cried. "What's happening?"

"Do not be afraid," came a voice. "We have come to tell you good news of great joy for all the people. Tonight a baby was born in Bethlehem. He is the Messiah, the Savior of the world!"

The shepherds were amazed. They wondered what they should do. And then the answer came.

"You will find the baby in Bethlehem. He is wrapped in bands of cloth and lying in a manger," the angel said. Then all the angels began to sing, "Glory to God, and peace to all the world."

"Did you hear that?" "What does it mean?" "Let's go to Bethlehem!" "Let's go see the Savior!" the excited shepherds all began to speak at once.

They gathered their things, planned for the care of their sheep, and began the trip to Bethlehem, where they found the newborn Jesus.

"Praise God," they said. "We must tell everyone about this wonderful thing. We must tell everyone that the Savior has come!"

Day 1
Draw a Christmas tree outline on construction paper and mark it off into six sections. Encourage family members to list the following on the tree (younger children may draw pictures or just decorate the tree): 1. List two gifts—one you received that you especially enjoyed and one special gift you gave to someone else. 2. List three things you are good at—special gifts that God has given you. 3. List two gifts you would like to receive for Christmas. Remember that feelings, talents, and experiences can be gifts. 4. Name a way you will use one of the gifts you have received (or will receive this year) to serve God or other people during the next year. 5. Name a gift you would like to give to God. 6. Write a special Christmas message to your family and friends. Add the papers to your "Wondrous Things" scrapbook.

Day 2
Enjoy candy canes while you hear this story. Once there was a candymaker who wanted to give his friends a special Christmas gift. After a while, as he looked at one of his ordinary candy sticks, he had an idea. While the candy was still warm, the candy-maker bent the top over until the stick looked like a shepherd's crook. "This is it," he exclaimed. "This candy stick looks like a shepherd's crook. If I make candy like this for my friends, my gift will remind them of the shepherds who were the first ones to hear about Jesus' birth."

Day 3
Take a trip to the library to find books on various Christmas customs (or use the Internet). How did your favorite custom originate?

Day 4
Cut out hearts. Print the following message on the hearts before decorating them: "God loves you so much that God sent Jesus." Send the hearts to special friends, or take them to a nursing home or homeless shelter.

Day 5
Act out the story of the shepherds on the hillside. Encourage family members to show the fear, awe, and excitement the shepherds must have felt.

Day 6
Look through Christmas cards. Talk about the meanings of the symbols you see—stars, mangers, shepherds, and doves.

Day 7
Talk about Santa Claus. No matter what your child thinks about Santa Claus, help him or her to separate Santa Claus from the celebration of Jesus' birth. However, help your child to understand too that Santa Claus is a reminder of goodwill and the spirit of giving.

Led by a Star

Talk Point:
Wise men came from far away to worship Jesus and to bring him gifts. Christians today can help people know that Jesus is God's gift to everyone.

Many years ago, even before Jesus was born in Bethlehem, some wise men from the East had been watching the sky to learn about the world. Then one night a very bright star appeared in the heavens. They knew that the star was a special sign. It was a sign that a king had been born.

Quickly the wise men gathered supplies and gifts. They began a trip in the direction of the star. They wanted to find this special king. When they came to Jerusalem, they went to King Herod to ask, "Where is the child who has been born King of the Jews? We have seen his star, and we have come to honor him."

Herod was very upset! How could there be a child who would be king? Herod was the king! The news the men from the East brought frightened Herod. Immediately he called all the religious leaders together. "Where is the Messiah to be born?" he commanded them to tell him.

"In Bethlehem, according to the prophet," they answered.

"Go quickly," Herod said to the wise men. "Find this child who will be king. And when you have found him, come quickly to tell me so that I may come to worship him too." But the truth was that Herod wanted to know where the baby was so that he could keep the baby from becoming king.

When the wise men left the palace, the star started moving to help them find their way. When it stopped, they knew that they had found the child they had been searching for. They were overwhelmed with joy!

When the wise men went into the house, they knelt and worshiped Jesus. They gave him wonderful gifts of gold, frankincense, and myrrh. The wise men were excited to know that they had found the baby who would become a special king.

That night while the wise men slept, they had a dream. They knew that they must not go back to Jerusalem to tell Herod how to find this child. They chose to return home by a different route so that they would not have to see Herod again.

Day 1 Continue to use library books and the Internet to find out what tradition says about the wise men. A good book to read would be *The Fourth Wiseman* (Dial Books for Young Readers, 1998). While certainly make believe, this story will help children see that making decisions to do the right thing cannot be put off.

Day 2 Decorate sugar cookies to share with someone. Use ready-made dough (or your favorite recipe) and star-shaped cookie cutters. Remind your child that the wise men followed the star and then shared the good news.

Day 3 Cover a small box with gold paper or aluminum foil. On scraps of construction paper have each family member write what gift he or she would like to give the Christ Child in the coming year. Keep the box on your kitchen table to remind you often.

Day 4 Talk about ways your family can honor Jesus by giving a gift to God through your church. Remind your family that gifts of time are as important as gifts of money.

Day 5 Epiphany, celebrated on January 6, is sometimes called Three Kings Day. Epiphany is the twelfth day of Christmas, a day for celebrating God's gift of Jesus to all people and the church's mission to spread the good news of God's love through all the world. In Puerto Rico children prepare a box of grass and a cup of water for the wise men's camels on the night of January 5. The next morning they hurry out to find the gifts that were left for them by the wise men. Adapt this tradition to your family, by making a card for an older person in your community and wishing them very best in the coming new year.

Day 6 Bake a Three Kings cake. Put a lima bean or an almond in the batter of your favorite cake. According to tradition, th person who finds the bean or almond is crowned king or queen for the day.

Day 7 In Norway and France children parade through the streets carrying a long pole with a lighted star at the top. Three children dress as the wise men; other children dress as shepherds, angels, and other characthers. Let your children have an Epiphany parade, dressing as their favorite characters. Invite them to tell the other family members why they chose their character.

Jesus Grew

When Jesus was born, Joseph and Mary were in Bethlehem, far away from their home in Nazareth. They had to come to Bethlehem to pay their taxes.

Jesus was not born in a warm house or even in an inn where travelers usually stayed. Joseph and Mary had found shelter in a place where animals were kept, because all the innkeepers had said, "Sorry, we're full. There's no room."

Joseph and Mary were glad to have a special baby to love and to care for. Later they traveled from Bethlehem to Jerusalem to take their new little baby to the Jewish Temple. "Our baby is special to us," Joseph said. "We want to make a promise to God that we will teach our new son to serve God."

Because Herod wanted to harm baby Jesus, his parents took him to live in Egypt for several years. Finally, Joseph and Mary were able to take their little boy home to Nazareth. Jesus grew strong and healthy. He played with his friends and helped his father in the carpenter shop.

When he was five, Jesus began to go to the synagogue school, where he learned to read and write. And when he was twelve years old, Joseph and Mary took him with them to Jerusalem. Now he was old enough to sit in the Temple and talk with the teachers there.

Jesus was so interested that he stayed behind to talk more with the teachers after Joseph and Mary had left. When his parents returned, Mary was upset. "Jesus, you worried us," she said. "We have been searching for you everywhere." Jesus was surprised. He thought they would have known he wanted to learn more about God.

After that Jesus was always careful to obey his parents. He grew to be an adult. He taught people about God. And he loved children.

All through his growing-up years and even when he was grown, Jesus was always eager to learn new things. He was always helpful to his friends and neighbors. He wanted to serve God as his parents had promised he would when he was just a baby.

Day 1 Talk about how Jesus' study of the Scriptures in the synagogue is similar to experiences of learning in school and Sunday school today. Try to find children's books about life in Bible times that will show how the boys wrote their letters first in the sand, then on wax tablets, and so on. Explain that girls did not go to school at that time, but rather learned from their mothers the things they needed to know about running the house, going to the market to buy food, and caring for their family.

Day 2 Show your child his or her baby pictures. Talk about all the things your child can do now that were not possible as a baby (read, count, ride a bike, and so forth).

Day 3 Show some pictures of family members as a child and as a youth. Talk about growing up and changes that take place.

Day 4 If there is a synagogue in your community, drive by it. Remind your child that Jesus learned to read and write in a synagogue school. His family also worshiped in the synagogue, just as your family attends church to worship God.

Day 5 Jesus learned household tasks and carpentry skills from Mary and Joseph. Help your child learn some new skills. If possible, take your child to work with you. Show your child what you do.

Day 6 Share a Scripture with your child that has helped you to grow closer to God.

Day 7 Ask your child to share his or her favorite Bible verse with you. Encourage family members to write their favorite verses down to save in the "Wondrous Things" scrapbook.

Jesus Is Baptized

Talk Point:
John the Baptist helped people get ready to hear Jesus' message and to follow Jesus. We can get ready to be followers of Jesus.

Repent and be baptized," preached John to a large crowd of people who had gathered beside the Jordan River.

John was different from most of the people who had come to hear him. His clothes were made from camel's hair, and he wore a belt made from leather. John ate locusts (similar to grasshoppers) and wild honey. Crowds were coming from all of Judea and Jerusalem to see and hear this unusual preacher.

"Repent and be baptized," John said again. "Confess your sins. Tell God you are sorry for the wrong things you do. Change and start doing what is right."

The prophets had told of a messiah who would come to the people of Israel. So some may have understood when John continued, "Someone so great is coming that I am not worthy to take off his shoes. I can baptize you with water. But the powerful one who will come after me will baptize you with the Holy Spirit,"

John said, "Come out into this river and be baptized." And many people did just that.

One day while John was preaching, Jesus came to the Jordan River. Jesus asked John to baptize him. So the two men walked out into the water, and John baptized Jesus. As Jesus was coming out of the water, he saw the Spirit coming out of the heavens like a dove. And he heard a voice from heaven say, "You are my Son, my Beloved; with you I am well pleased."

We cannot be sure if anyone else saw the dove or heard the voice. But this day was an important one for Jesus, for he would soon begin teaching all who would listen about God's love.

Day 1

If your child was baptized or dedicated as an infant, talk with your child about the promise you made to bring him or her up in a Christian environment. Show your child any pictures or certificates that you may have kept. If your child has not been baptized, talk with him or her about your feelings about baptism. Answer questions about how he or she can make decisions about being baptized.

Day 2

Give your young child items such as cups, spoons, and sponges to play with in the tub. Recall stories about water that you have used in the past months. Remind your child of how important water is to all of God's creation. If your children are older, talk about what it means for your child to make his or her own commitment.

Day 3

Enjoy making and eating blue gelatin with your family. Point out that you are using water to make the gelatin. When the gelatin is ready to eat, talk about how the gelatin looks and tastes. Talk about how gelatin feels wet when you eat it.

Day 4

Talk with your child about the Christian responsibility to serve others. Choose a project you can work on together.

Day 5

Help your child remember how he or she learned to talk, to count, to ride a bike, to play the piano, and so forth. Then suggest that the way we learn to live as Jesus taught is the same. We learn by practicing. If you have a photo of one of these "first times," take it to a copy store and make an enlargement. Think of a clever caption that will remind family members that we grow through practice.

Day 6

Mix together 1/4 cup liquid detergent, 1/2 cup water, and 1 teaspoon sugar in a plastic tub or shallow bowl. Tear the bottoms of some paper cups. Dip the rims of the cups into the bubble solution and blow through the bottoms. Enjoy watching the bubbles.

Day 7

Let family members trace around their hands and then add an eye and a beak to the thumb to make a hand print dove. Write a favorite Bible verse on the doves and add them to your Wondrous Things scrapbook.

Follow Me!

Scripture:
Mark 1:16-20;
2:13-14; 3:13-19

Talk Point:

God sent Jesus into the world to bring good news to all people. Jesus called all kinds of people to follow him. Jesus calls us to be his disciples and to help with his work today.

One day as Jesus was walking along the Sea of Galilee, he saw Andrew and his brother Simon (whom Jesus later named Peter) fishing. Jesus called to them, "Follow me, and I will make you fish for people." Somehow Andrew and Simon knew that what Jesus was calling them to do was important. They immediately laid down their nets and followed Jesus.

As they continued to walk by the sea, they soon saw James and John with their father, Zebedee. The brothers were in a boat with their father. They were also fishermen, and they were mending their nets. When Jesus called to them, James and John put down what they were doing and followed Jesus.

On another day, when Jesus was teaching the people who had gathered near the sea, he saw Levi sitting nearby at a tax booth. Levi, who was sometimes called Matthew, was a lonely man. Tax collectors were often dishonest people, and the crowds did not trust Matthew. But Jesus and his followers stopped to speak to the tax collector. "Levi," Jesus said, "follow me." And to the surprise of those who were nearby, Levi immediately left his work and followed Jesus. In fact, Levi was so excited that he invited Jesus to eat at his house that night. There other tax collectors and sinners met Jesus.

Soon many people were following Jesus. Many of them were women—Mary Magdalene, Joanna, Susanna, Mary and Martha, and Jesus' own mother, Mary, followed Jesus. Soon Jesus decided to choose twelve of those who were following him to be his special helpers. These twelve we know as the apostles.

Jesus spent a great deal of time with the twelve apostles. Jesus taught them what they needed to know to help teach others about God's love. The twelve Jesus chose were Peter and his brother Andrew, the brothers James and John, Matthew, Philip, Bartholomew, Thomas, another James (whose father's name was Alphaeus), Thaddaeus, another apostle named Simon, and Judas Iscariot.

Day 1 Make prayer cards for your table. Fold a sheet of construction paper in half to make a tent card. Encourage each family member to write a prayer about how your family can be disciples. Use these prayers at family times. Use ordinary dry kitchen sponges. Cut several fish shapes from each sponge. Dilute one part food coloring in a foil pie plate with five parts water. Prepare several colors. Carefully dip one side of the fish-shaped sponge into the food color. Tap the sponge gently on the side of the pie plate to remove the excess color. Press the sponge lightly on each side of the prayer card to decorate around the prayer.

Day 2 Use kitchen scissors to cut bread into the shape of fish for sandwiches or toast. Let a younger child retell the story of Jesus calling the fishermen while you enjoy the food.

Day 3 Encourage each family member to make a disciple calendar to follow for a week. On a sheet of construction paper list the days of the week. Leave a space following each day. Decorate any way you wish. Each day think of one way you can be a disciple

Day 4 Ask each family member to tell the others what he or she thinks it means to be one of Jesus' followers. Help one another think of ways to serve others in Jesus' name.

Day 5 Choose Bible stories about followers of Jesus to read at bedtime. Read from a colorful Bible storybook so that all the details will be easy for younger children to follow.

Day 6 Cut out fish shapes to place on your refrigerator. Each time your child shows love toward God or others, name the deed and draw a smile, eye, or other decoration on the fish. Add the fish to your "Wondrous Things" scrapbook when you are finished.

Day 7 If you are not already involved in a service project, choose one with your children. Suggest giving a toy to a community shelter, making cookies for Sunday school teachers, cleaning up the churchyard, reading a book to a younger child, or some other simple project your children can do. Encourage each child to see his or her acts of kindness as following Jesus by loving as Jesus taught us to love.

Teach Us to Pray

Scripture:
Mark 1:35; 6:41, 46;
14:22-23
Luke 11:1-4

Talk Point:

Jesus prayed and taught his disciples to pray. We can pray, telling God our thoughts and asking for God's help.

Jesus liked to talk to God in prayer. That is what prayer is. When we pray, we tell God our thoughts and our feelings. In prayer we can ask God to help us. And in prayer we listen to know what God wants to say to us.

Jesus spent a great deal of time in prayer. Sometimes he would pray all night. Sometimes he would get up very early and go into the mountains to be alone with God.

One of the special times when Jesus prayed was to say a prayer of thanks to God before eating. One day more than five thousand people were with Jesus, listening to him teach. When it got late in the day, they became hungry. On that day Jesus took a little boy's lunch and gave thanks to God for the food. After Jesus had blessed the food, there was enough for everyone to eat.

Again, when Jesus ate his last meal with his disciples on the night he was arrested, he asked God to bless the food. Then Jesus and his friends ate together. On this night Jesus told his disciples to remember him always whenever they gathered to eat together.

The disciples often saw Jesus praying. One day they stayed close by while Jesus was praying alone. When Jesus had finished praying, one of the disciples said, "Lord, teach us to pray."

Jesus was glad to teach his disciples a simple prayer that would help them speak to God. Jesus said, "When you pray, say: "Father, hallowed be your name, your kingdom come. Give us each day our daily bread. Forgive us our sins, for we also forgive everyone who sins against us. And lead us not into temptation."

Today we call Jesus' prayer the Lord's Prayer. There are several versions of the prayer. You probably do not say the prayer in your church exactly the way it is printed in the Bible. Pray the Lord's Prayer today in the way that is most familiar to you.

Day 1

There are five kinds of prayer. To help your family remember them, talk about ACTS plus I. A is for adoration or praise—we recognize how great God is and we say how much we love God.
C is for confession—to confess is to tell God that we know we have done things that are wrong. T is for thanksgiving—we recognize what God has given to us and done for us. We say, "Thank you, God." S is for supplication or petition—we tell God what we need. I is for intercession—we pray for someone else. Through prayers of intercession we may ask God to help someone, to comfort someone, or to be present with someone during a difficult time.

Day 2

Look up the following Bible reference about prayer. Ask "When? Where? Why? How?" questions about each: Mark 1:35; Luke 6:12; 18:10; Acts 10:9; 16:23-25; Philippians 1:3-4; and James 5:16.

Day 3

One of the most important kinds of prayer is praying for others (intercession). Let your family know that you are praying for each family member. Encourage each family member to pray for others each day. If you do not already pray before meals, start that practice now.

Day 4

Compare the Lord's Prayer as it is written in Luke 11:2-4 with the way it is written in Matthew 6:9-13. Suggest that as a family you write your own version of the Lord's Prayer in words that have meaning to you.

Day 5

Help each child choose one of the five ways of praying and draw a picture to illustrate it. Add to your "Wondrous Things" scrapbook.

Day 6

Make a big poster that says, "Thank You, God!" Each day add one thing to the poster for which your family thanks God.

Day 7

Use a concordance to see how many times prayer appears in the Bible. Look up some of the references and decide what kind of prayer they are.

Jesus Heals

Talk Point:
Jesus cared about sick people and healed many of them. We can love and care for persons who are sick or hurt or who have a disability.

Something unusual happened the other day. I was there. I saw and heard everything, but I can hardly believe it even now. I don't know what to think about it.

I'm a Pharisee, a religious leader among the Jewish people outside of Jerusalem. There are a lot of us. We have spent our lives studying the Jewish Law and telling others what it means. We have become well-known for how carefully we respect the Law and carry it out down to the last detail.

Well, we'd been hearing a lot about this man called Jesus. He was going about our towns and cities teaching, preaching, and even healing people, so we thought we'd better check him out. We had heard where he was going to be that day, so several of us Pharisees gathered at the house where he was teaching.

I listened carefully to what he said. He was an amazing teacher. Then while he was speaking, I noticed a commotion in the crowd outside.

Four men, carrying a fifth man on a pallet, were trying to press their way through to Jesus. Too many people were crowded into that small space. There was no way they were going to get through. I soon forgot about them and turned my attention back to Jesus.

The next thing we heard was a lot of noise on the roof. Can you believe it? Those men had climbed up on the roof and were making a hole in it. When the hole was large enough, they lowered their friend's pallet to the floor right in front of Jesus!

It was clear that the man couldn't walk. He must have been like that for a long time—maybe even all his life. We watched to see what Jesus would do.

What Jesus said next shocked us. He looked at the man and told him that his sins were forgiven. We Pharisees couldn't believe our ears. Only God can forgive sins. Did this Jesus think he was God?

We were muttering among ourselves. Jesus looked right at us. "Which is easier," he asked, "to say, 'Your sins are forgiven you,' or to say, 'Stand up and walk'?"

Then he told the man to stand up, take up his pallet, and go home. And the man did! I still can't believe it. The man who was healed glorified God, and so did we. What an amazing day!

Day 1 Make cards for someone (or more than one person) who is sick. As a family go to visit the person (if it is appropriate) during the week.

Day 2 Talk about the skills God gives to doctors and nurses. Give thanks together for them and for hospitals and medicines that help people get well.

Day 3 Read a storybook about modern health care. Your librarian should have several to suggest. If you have older children who enjoy looking things up on the Internet, think of various topics related to health care and have them research the topics.

Day 4 Visit a nursing home with your child. Consider making visits on a regular basis.

Day 5 Work together on a thank-you note or drawing to send to your child's doctor.

Day 6 Ask your child is there are children with disabilities at his or her school. Encourage your child to be a friend to those children with special needs.

Day 7 Ask your grocer for a medium-sized box. Cut out two sides of the box to create a lap table to use in bed the next time someone in the family is sick. Decorate the box together.

New Commandment

Scripture:
Mark 12:28-34
John 13:34-35
Deuteronomy 6:4-9

Talk Point:

Jesus taught that the most important commandments are to love God and neighbor. We can learn to love and care for others.

So many questions! The people had so many questions to ask Jesus! One day a scribe who was standing nearby overheard Jesus talking to some of the religious leaders. He was interested in what Jesus had to say, so he asked Jesus, "Which commandment is the most important of all the commandments?"

Jesus quickly answered, "The greatest of the commandments is one you know well. It is: 'Hear O Israel: the Lord our God, the Lord is one; you shall love the Lord your God with all your heart, and with all your soul, and with all your mind, and with all your strength.'"

The scribe certainly did know that commandment. It was a verse from Deuteronomy that the Hebrew people repeated several times every day. This verse was so important to them that they were instructed to teach it to their children. They also wrote the verse down and kept it in a little box at their doorways so that they could touch it each time they entered their houses. They also wore the verse in a little box tied around their forehead or on their upper left arm. The verse was with them every day when they prayed.

But Jesus was not finished. Jesus quickly continued, "The second commandment is this, 'You shall love your neighbor as yourself.' There is no other commandment greater than these."

"Yes," said the scribe, "you are right. To love God with all your heart, understanding, and strength, and to love your neighbor as yourself is greater than anything else we can do, including all the sacrifices."

Jesus was pleased with the scribe's understanding. "Oh! You are very close to God's kingdom," he said to the scribe.

Not long after that Jesus was eating the Last Supper with his disciples. Once again he told them about the important commandment to love one another. Jesus said to them, "I give you a new commandment, that you love one another. Just as I have loved you, you should love one another."

Jesus was clear about the most important commandments. Jesus taught that above all else his followers must love God. And Jesus knew that others would recognize his followers because of the love they showed one another and others. "By this love everyone will know that you are my disciples, if you have love for one another," he told them. Jesus knew that seeing the disciples loving and serving would make others want to be disciples too.

Day 1 Let your children help plan something special your family can do together to show your love for someone who needs extra love right now. Pray for this person together.

Day 2 Make a family "Love Gallery." Cover a large piece of cardboard with wrapping paper and mount pictures of friends and family members on it. Write "Love Gallery" on it and display it where your children can enjoy it.

Day 3 Remind your family that God is always doing new things. Together plant some flower seeds in a pot on a sunny windowsill. Water, wait, and watch to see the new thing that God does. Do you have a neighbor who would enjoy the plant?

Day 4 Read 1 Corinthians 13 with your older child. Talk about what love is and what love is not according to the Bible passage. Talk about ways each of you can show love in your family, with your friends, and in your community.

Day 5 Help your child understand that a neighbor is more than just the person who lives next door. A neighbor is any person in need. What can your family do to help someone in need in your community? Children learn by watching your example as well as by participating in loving deeds of service. If your church supports a missionary, take time to write to that person or family now. If possible, enclose a small gift of remembrance.

Day 6 Work together to memorize the Great Commandment and the second commandment. Say them together at mealtime.

Day 7 Jesus gave his disciples the second commandment during the feast of the Passover. Recall with your children the stories of Moses leading the children of Israel out of Egypt. Re-read those stories from Bible storybooks. Find out more about the feast of the Passover from library books or the Internet.

A Long, Dark Night

Scripture:
Mark 14:32-50
John 18:10-11

Talk Point:

In Gethsemane Jesus prayed that God's will would be done in his life. We can pray and ask God to help us live as God wants us to live.

It was the darkest part of the night. Peter pulled his woolen cloak close. Strange, how bright the stars were! Peter could see Jesus as clearly as if a lamp were lit. Peter looked around at the gnarled trunks of olive trees and the shocked, staring faces of James and John.

Peter knew how James and John felt. He too had felt sick and scared since Jesus had told them that he would die, having been betrayed and deserted by his own disciples! Peter had said he, at least, would never leave Jesus. Jesus had replied, "Peter, before daybreak, you will have said three times you never knew me."

Peter had sputtered, but now he began to feel doubt creep in. *I'm too young to die. Can I stand the pain? Why don't we just leave Jerusalem?* Peter pushed the thoughts away, muttering, "I love Jesus. I will stay with him." The doubts stopped for a moment. Then they bubbled up again.

The disciples had never seen such sadness in Jesus' face. Jesus said, "Stay awake here while I pray." He went off, but not far. They could hear him clearly. "Abba, Father, for you all things are possible. Take this cup from me. Yet let it be as you want, not as I want." Peter closed his eyes to pray too, but he was so terribly tired! Suddenly he was awakened by Jesus' voice. "Peter, couldn't you keep awake for an hour? Pray not to be tested!"

Peter sat up. Jesus left again to pray. Peter dug his nails into his palms, hoping the pain would keep him awake. But the next thing he knew, Jesus was shaking him again. "Are you still sleeping?" Jesus asked. "Enough! It's time! Here comes my betrayer!"

In a moment the night was loud with voices. Judas darted from a crowd of soldiers and Temple guards. He ran to Jesus and kissed him. Peter drew his sword. He knew that he could never fight them and win. But he took a swipe with the sword anyway and cut off the ear of the high priest's slave. Then he ran away with James and John, leaving Jesus alone, a prisoner.

And as he went, Peter was sobbing. "I didn't know! I didn't know! I didn't know it would be so hard to follow Jesus!" But no one heard him.

Day 1 Go to the library to look for a book of prayers. Learn a new prayer to say at bedtime.

Day 2 Make a paper chain with one word of a prayer written on each link. Hang the chain where your family can see it. Occasionally stop and read the prayer together.

Day 3 Look in the newspaper for a community planting or cleanup project to participate in. Encourage your family to give time together to help your community. Remind your child of Jesus' prayer in Gethsemane: ". . . not what I want, but what you want."

Day 4 Read Mark 14:26-31, 66-72 with your older children. Talk about why Peter denied he knew Jesus. Ask your child if it is hard for him or her to admit to friends and schoolmates that Jesus is important to him or her. Encourage your child to talk about some of the pressures of school life, and be open to what he or she has to say. Close with a prayer together for all your child's friends. Pray that they will come to know how precious they are to God.

Day 5 Read and discuss Mark 14:32-50 with your older child. Ask questions that you both have ideas about. Why do you suppose the disciples fell asleep so much? Why didn't Jesus just leave Jerusalem if he knew all those people were coming to get him? Why did Peter leave Jesus after saying he would not?

Day 6 Write Jesus' prayer from Mark 14:36 across a page. See how many words you can come up with using the letters in the prayer. Letters can be reused, but not in a single word. For example, you only have one c available per word because there is only one c in the prayer.

Day 7 Work together to make up a prayer for courage in scary situations. Write the prayer down and say it together until you all know it by heart.

Jesus Is Alive!

Scripture:
Matthew 27:1-2, 31, 50;
28:1-10

Talk Point:
Jesus' resurrection shows God's love and God's gift of new life. At Easter we celebrate with joy and hope.

It was the saddest of all days! It was the day hundreds of shouting people had followed Jesus to a cross. Jesus, the one who had come to teach about God's love and to do God's will, was dying.

"Jesus can't bother us anymore!" they said. Almost everyone thought this was the end of Jesus' work. Even most of his followers thought their dreams were ended.

But only three days later, it was the happiest of all days! It was the morning after the sabbath, the day of rest. Darkness still covered the land as Mary Magdalene and Mary rushed to Jesus' tomb.

When they got there, the earth suddenly began to shake violently. An angel of the Lord came and rolled the stone back from the entrance to Jesus' grave. When the women saw the angel sitting on the stone, they were surprised.

"Don't be afraid," the angel said. "You are looking for Jesus. But he is not here. He has been raised. He is alive! Go as fast as you can to the disciples. Tell them that Jesus is alive."

The sun's rays were shining on the road as the women hurried away. They were laughing and both talking at once in their excitement. They weren't paying attention to the people they passed along the way.

Then all at once a man stood in front of them. They had not seen him coming toward them.

"Greetings!" he said.

They could never forget that voice. "It is Jesus!" they both said as they fell on their knees, hugging his feet.

I am sure Jesus touched them on their heads as he said, "Do not be afraid. Go to the disciples. Tell them that I will meet them in Galilee."

What an awesome day! What a wonderful day! What a happy day! Jesus was alive!

Day 1 Share a special Easter tradition. When two people meet, the first says, "Christ is risen!" the second replies, "Christ is risen indeed!" Use this greeting at breakfast this week. Take turns being the first speaker, with everyone else saying the second part together.

Day 2 Talk with your family about persons in your family or friends who have physically died. If your children have questions, answer them. Talk about what you believe it means to be with God.

Day 3 Visit the graves of people your family has known. If possible, leave a flower to remind yourselves of the hope that you will see one another again.

Day 4 Put together a small spring basket of flowers to take to an elderly friend. Look for an Easter basket on sale. Buy or make the flowers unless you have some blooming in your yard or garden.

Day 5 Talk about how the tradition of wearing new clothes at Easter got started. In the early Chruch, new Christians were baptized at Easter. After they were baptized, they were given a new, white robe to symbolize their new life in Christ.

Day 6 Listen to some Easter music from contemporary Christian artists. Compare the words of the songs to older hymns with which your family is familiar. Do any of the songs remind us of the promise God made to God's people?

Day 7 Make up an Easter dance. Take turns choreographing the moves.

Go and Tell

Scripture:
Matthew 28:16-20
Luke 24:50-52

Talk Point:
Jesus sent his followers out to tell the good news and to teach. As Jesus' followers we find ways to tell the good news about Jesus.

Jesus had told the disciples he would meet them on a mountain in Galilee. It was a beautiful day. The disciples went where Jesus had told them to go. Suddenly Jesus appeared. The disciples were excited! They worshiped Jesus. They told him how much they loved him and how happy they were to see him.

But some of the disciples doubted. Could this really be Jesus? Had he come back to see them again? They really didn't understand. But somehow they knew that Jesus was alive.

Jesus said, "I have all power. I want you to go into all the world. I want you to help others become my disciples. Everyone should learn about me just as you learned about me."

Jesus wanted them to teach and preach the good news. They were to baptize people who believed in Jesus. Jesus wanted these new believers to follow Jesus' way and to obey Jesus' rules.

Then Jesus said, "Remember, I will be with you forever and forever. Go and tell."

Then Jesus left them just as quickly as he had come. Jesus blessed the disciples. As Jesus gave them God's peace, he was taken to heaven in a cloud.

The disciples were full of joy. They went back to Jerusalem. They knew they could go and tell the good news. They knew that Jesus was alive.

Day 1 Learn the verse Matthew 28:19 together and talk together about what the verse can mean for your family.

Day 2 Recall together what the term *gospel* means (good news). Put together a family newspaper or newsletter telling how God has worked in your lives and things for which you are thankful. Encourage family members to draw pictures as well as to write stories. Take the paper to a photocopying service and share copies with relatives and friends.

Day 3 Talk about ways people in your area are telling the good news. Talk about local outreach ministries such as soup kitchens, food pantries, used clothing stores, literacy programs, work with people who are homeless, help for people who are abused, and other programs.

Day 4 Encourage your family to adopt an unchurched family in your community. Talk about ways that each of you can reach out to that family with acts of kindness and words of encouragement.

Day 5 Invite your pastor's family to come to your house for an evening of fellowship, fun, and snacks.

Day 6 Read 1 Thessalonians 5:11. How can we build up other people? How does love help? Make a poster of building blocks (if a member of your family is talented artistically, add some tools used in building). On each block, write one thing your family can do to encourage someone else. If you wish, make a small poster to add to your "Wondrous Things" scrapbook.

Day 7 Spend an evening looking back through your "Wondrous Things" scrapbook. Which activities did your family enjoy most? Pray, thanking God for families. Plan what you will do for devotions in the coming year.

1. Prepare at least 9 promise coupons. (Fill in a specific promise on at least 5 of the coupons. The other coupons may be left blank until you decide what promises you want to make.)
2. Stack your promise coupons neatly with the cover on the top.
3. Staple the coupon book on the left side.
4. Choose someone to receive each promise. When you make a promise, tear a coupon out of the book and give it to the person to whom the promise is made.
5. Try to make and keep all nine of your promises during the next week.

COVER

PROMISE COUPONS

I promise
_____
_____
Signed _____

I promise
_____
_____
Signed _____

I promise
_____
_____
Signed _____

I promise
_____
_____
Signed _____

I promise
_____
_____
Signed _____

I promise
_____
_____
Signed _____

I promise
_____
_____
Signed _____

I promise
_____
_____
Signed _____

I promise
_____
_____
Signed _____

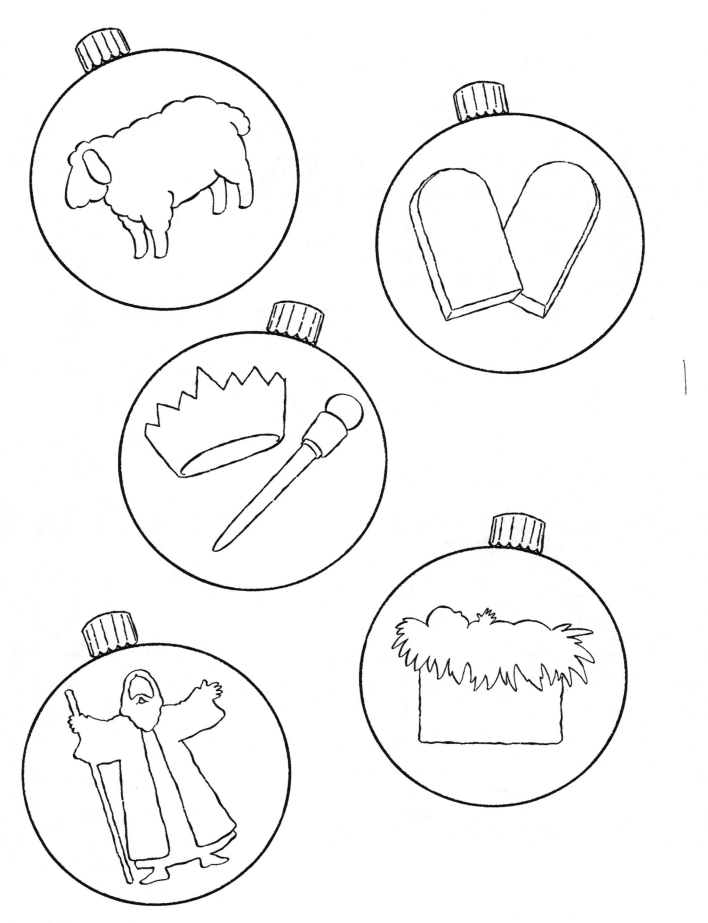

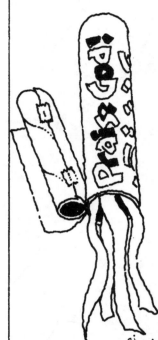

save

1. Decorate your cover for a celebration streamer. Use bright colors!
2. Tape several colors of crepe paper streamers around the edge of one end of a paper towel tube.
3. Cover the tube with the cover you have prepared.
4. Wave your streamer as you praise God.

ORSS, © 1998 Abingdon Press; Art: Susan Harrison